From
Hawks to
Hummingbirds

A complimentary copy of this book is provided by:

THE CONSERVATION FUND

America's Partner in Conservation

TYRRELL COUNTY
Eco Tourism
NORTH CAROLINA

www.palmettopeartree.com

www.visittyrrellcounty.com

From Hawks to Hummingbirds

Close Encounters with Birds of the North Carolina Coastal Plain

PARIS TRAIL

with illustrations by Deb Kozlowski

SWEET BAY TREE BOOKS
Columbia, NC

Dedication
to DOROTHY
who puts up with my gypsy ways
and tries to keep me scheduled.

Acknowledgements
I would like to thank my "bird buddies:"
all the people who keep me informed
of strange birds at the feeder;
particularly Fred Inglis.

The text of this book
originally appeared in *The Chowan Herald*
as the series 'A Country Journal'
and in *The Roanoke Beacon*
as 'A Countryman's Journal.'

This collection edited & first published in 1997
by Sweet Bay Tree Books, Columbia, NC

Library of Congress Catalog Number 97-68915
ISBN 0-9643396-1-7

Printed & bound in the USA
by Professional Press, Chapel Hill

Contents

* all illustrations by Deb Kozlowski
except Tree Sparrow & Pileated Woodpecker
(Paris Trail)

PARIS TRAIL

Born on a farm near Grafton, Virginia, Paris grew up in rural settings in Virginia and Pennsylvania, where he developed his life-long interest in the natural world. When World War II broke out he enlisted and served with the navy in the Pacific. Always a source of puzzlement to his ship-mates, he usually headed for parks and the countryside on shore leave instead of the fleshpots which were the destinations of most of the crew. At the end of the war he attended the Rochester Institute of Technology, graduating two years later with an Associate Degree in Photography. In 1955, after a spell as a photographer at the US Naval Proving Ground in Virginia, he accepted a position as Photographer and Visual Aids Tech-nologist at Cornell University's NYS Agricultural Experiment Station in Geneva, New York. He and his wife Dorothy bought a hundred-acre farm in Clifton Springs and settled down for the next twenty-eight years. They raised four children—daughters Robin and Toby and sons Pepper and Matt, who later produced three grandchildren—Graham, Lark, and Sage.

In 1983 Paris retired, and after a year of searching he and Dorothy moved to Edenton, a small town in the North Carolina Coastal Plain. From their home in the middle of ten acres of mature deciduous trees, Paris sets out almost every day with camera and pen, recording and interpreting the flora and fauna of the region. A member of the Stewardship Committee of the Nature Conservancy and State Parks, he conducts field observations on bats for the NC State Museum and is involved in research on breeding birds. Well known as an artist and wood-sculptor and very active in the Chowan Arts Council, he is also a keen golfer and occasional fisherman. His bi-monthly nature column is carried by two newspapers, the Chowan Herald and the Roanoke Beacon, from which he has compiled this account of his adventures with the birds of the area during the eleven years from 1985 to 1996.

DEB KOZLOWSKI

Illustrator Deb Kozlowski was born with a love of all creatures and all weeds and wild places. She has an undergraduate degree in Forestry from the University of New Hampshire and a Master's of Science in Soil Morphology from the University of Massachusetts. She has also studied animal science, chemistry, dressage riding, graphic design, surveying, apiculture, and several handcrafts, and has illustrated many university and Cooperative Extension Service publications in New Hampshire.

Deb, her husband David Lindbo, and son Duncan live on a small farm north of Edenton. She teaches at Pocosin Arts, a private, non-profit, educational organization connecting culture to environment through art, in Columbia, North Carolina.

At Home with Birds

AROUND THE FEEDER & IN THE WOODS

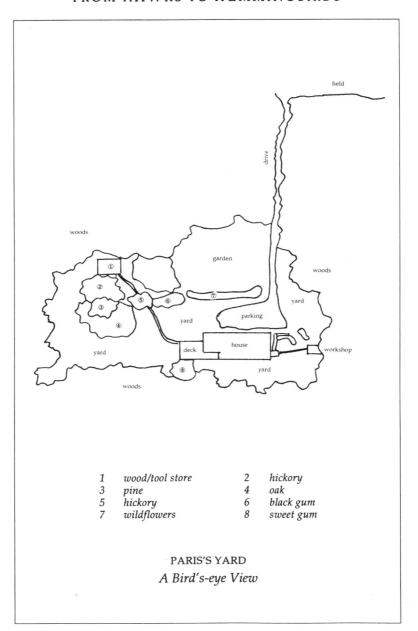

1	wood/tool store	2	hickory
3	pine	4	oak
5	hickory	6	black gum
7	wildflowers	8	sweet gum

PARIS'S YARD
A Bird's-eye View

BIRDS EVERYWHERE FOLLOW NATURAL CYCLES.
In the tropics bird activity mirrors the annual wet and dry seasons, while in the Northern Hemisphere it's the seasonal change from warm to cold and long to short days which affects avian behavior patterns. As the north grows cold and the days short, life either adapts or leaves. Most birds leave, gradually moving south as the days shorten, some eventually reaching the tropics. As the earth tilts, the days begin to get longer, the north starts to warm up, and the birds head north again to take advantage of the longer days and glut of insects to breed and raise their young. Bird migrations are driven by day length, not temperature, so their arrivals and departures are pretty predictable each year. From my own perch in the countryside near Edenton I follow the annual migrations with the greatest of interest.

Our ten acres comprise about the last mature upland hardwood forest in Chowan County. Directly to the east is another twenty acres or so of the same type of woods but only about sixty years old. Our woods were logged about a hundred years ago but not clearcut. A lot of big beech and some big hickories were left standing, and the woods now are comprised of big beech, most of them hollow, big oaks, hickories, yellow poplar, a big persimmon or two, a few sweet gums, big maples, and three dozen or so big loblolly pines. The understory is dogwood, hornbeam, and a few hollies. Nesting birds include wood thrush, ovenbirds, vireos, chickadees, titmice, nuthatches, downy and red-bellied woodpeckers, flickers, pileated woodpeckers, horned, barred, and screech-owls, wood-pewees, great-crested and Acadian flycatchers, and wood ducks. In the woods right around our yard I find at least four ruby-throated hummingbird nests each year.

The comings and goings of the birds in my yard and around the feeder are a constant source of fascination and pleasure. It is a joy each year to note the arrival of the first returning birds, and to follow the frantic activities of nesting and hatching the young. As the last migratory bird leaves at the end of the season, it's time to remove the nesting boxes and put up the feeders for the hardy birds which are our constant companions throughout the year. There's never a rest period for the dedicated birder!

11th July 1985

I finally mowed my back-yard meadow. Apart from violets it had a few primroses and a lot of sow thistles. When the thistles went to seed, hummingbirds began to gather the thistle for their nests and I was able to locate one nest back in the woods about thirty yards from the deck. I have my Celestron telescope with a 42-power eyepiece* focused on the nest and can watch all the activity as if it were only about three feet away! The two eggs have hatched and the female is busy feeding the young. The male is a carefree-bachelor type and takes no part in nest building or raising the family—he just spends his time chasing after females and sipping nectar. I have a hummingbird feeder by the deck, and about six females and three males visit it constantly. They are all rubythroats, the only species we have in the east, and are very pugnacious.

25th July 1985

The view from my deck is becoming more interesting as the summer progresses. I can see nests of the red-bellied woodpecker, northern flicker, wood-pewee, wood thrush, Acadian flycatcher, Carolina wren, and summer tanager, as well as three ruby-throated hummingbirds' nests. A mass of cardinal flowers along the edge of the woods is starting to bloom, and when the sun hits them the red color is dazzling. The hummingbirds have discovered them now and zoom from the feeder to the flowers. They really put on quite an aerial show around the feeder, hovering, dive-bombing, and lots of dog-fighting.

10th October 1985

This past summer I've had three rather interesting encounters with the barred owl which lives in my woods. This particular owl is not as wary as most. I hear it calling a lot, but met it for the

---

* The Celestron is actually an astronomical telescope, but with an erecting prism in its eyepiece it is a fine instrument for the close observation of all kinds of wildlife.

first time in March. I was sitting on a downed tree about half an hour before dusk when an owl came gliding through the woods and lit near me. It saw me, but as I sat motionless it soon dismissed me as harmless. It was obviously hunting, and I watched with binoculars as it investigated several small hollow stubs in a hornbeam tree. From one it extracted a small frog and promptly gulped it down. It sat quietly for perhaps fifteen minutes, turning its head sharply towards sounds I couldn't hear or perhaps sights I couldn't see (its night vision is one hundred times better than mine). It then glided across in front of me and pounced on something in the leaves. I could hear the thump it made as its feet hit the ground. It did a little dance in the leaves for a few seconds, then flew off carrying something small, probably a mouse.

I saw it again in August when I surprised it either taking a bath or trying to catch a frog or snake in the small pool where the culvert runs under my driveway. It was about the only water left in the woods. Frogs congregate there and red-bellied water snakes hunt the frogs. Coming back to the house it's on the driver's side, and I always coast up to it silently to see what's going on in it. This time the owl was almost belly deep in the water. We looked at each other from about ten feet for about a minute before it flew up to some branches a little way down the ditch. It apparently did not regard the car as dangerous or even particularly alarming. As a matter of fact, I often use the car as a blind. Most birds and animals are not alarmed by the car, and I take a lot of photographs with the telephoto lens resting on a beanbag on the car window.

The third time I saw the owl was two days before Hurricane Gloria. I was sitting on the deck with the binoculars when several squirrels began to scold in the edge of the woods. I didn't see anything alarming, and the cat and dog were both in the house, so I thought perhaps a large rat snake was causing all the fuss.

BARRED OWL
Strix varia

Then I saw the owl land in a tree about thirty yards from the deck. It appeared to be interested in something in the vines around the tree trunk. With the binoculars I saw first one then two more half-grown squirrels spiralling around the trunk with the owl in clumsy pursuit. The owl lit on a branch close to the trunk, peering for the young squirrels, who had frozen against the trunk. Several adult squirrels were still scolding nearby. To my amazement, one of the adults came jumping from branch to branch through the trees, landed on the end of the branch the owl was on, and jumped right at the owl's back. The owl flew to another branch, and the squirrel ran up and chased it entirely out of the tree. This was either a mother squirrel defending her young or a squirrel bent on committing suicide. Barred owls are supposed to catch and eat squirrels, but as male owls weigh about one pound and females a pound and a half, they would probably have trouble subduing an adult squirrel. I shall try to locate the owl's nesting tree in late February.

7th November 1985

Saturday I spent the afternoon and evening out in my workshop at the edge of the woods. I finished what I was working on at about 9 PM, turned out the light, and started for the house. Then, a short distance back in the woods, two bloodcurdling screams broke out, followed in a few seconds by several guttural hoots, then the familiar *Who cooks for you, Who cooks for you all.* Just my friend the barred owl letting me know he's still around an keeping an eye on things. When he has a mind to, he can really make the hair on the back of your neck rise up.

9th January 1986

Activity at my feeder is picking up. I have chickadees, towhees, juncos, white-throated sparrows, white-breasted nuthatches, blue jays, red-bellied woodpeckers, and a downy woodpecker actually using the feeder, and hanging around it are several flickers, pileated woodpeckers, and a small covey of quail. I suspect I have several nocturnal visitors too.

23rd January 1986

The Ojibwa Indians of the Canadian north woods call this time of year "the time of deep snow and long silence," but it's quite a different story here in coastal North Carolina.

I was awakened Monday morning by a terrific rapping which vibrated through the house like a riveting hammer. It seems a flicker had decided to use the weather-boarding on the corner of the house as a sounding board and was announcing to rival males that this was his territory. In fact, I wake up every bright sunny morning to the sounds of flickers, downy woodpeckers, red-bellied woodpeckers, and pileated woodpeckers, all busy at their favorite drumming stations on dead branches, hollow trees—or the corner of my house! The purpose of all this racket is to say "Keep out!" to other males of their species, and "Come and look me over!" to the females. It's a little early for this to be too serious yet, but the lengthening days are rousing dormant instincts. A pair of red-bellied woodpeckers who raised two broods in the dying maple in my back yard are excavating a hole about six feet below the old nest. Farther down, a smaller hole is also being excavated; from its size it looks like a downy woodpecker hole. It will be interesting to see how they sort it out. Red-bellied woodpeckers are not good neighbors: they have been known to prey on the young of other hole-nesters.

20th February 1986

My bird feeder is now a scene of frenzied activity as flocks of purple finches have finally located it and swarm in for sunflower seeds. I had two fox sparrows for several days last week, and have put up a thistle sock to entice goldfinches and pine siskins. The birds have gone through forty pounds of seed the last two weeks.

6th March 1986

One of the half dozen or so white-breasted nuthatches that visit my feeder has been gathering nesting material on the ground under the feeder, zooming around the corner of the house, and disappearing into the woods. I'm not sure how serious she is about it yet. It's hard to single her out from all the others who are constantly at the feeder, and when she suddenly picks up a bit of dead grass and takes off around the house it's still harder to get to the door in time to see where she's going with it. I'll find out eventually, if it takes me all day to do it!

Bluebirds are another March nester. The March 1986 issue of *Virginia Wildlife* has an article on about twenty birds who nest in March in Virginia and the Carolinas.

24th April 1986

The chickadees, nuthatches, titmice, and I have a little game going. They come to my feeders for sunflower seeds, and I try to follow them when they leave so I can locate their nests. So far they are winning! All three species are hole-nesters, and hundreds of acres of hardwoods behind my house have lots of old trees with lots of holes. I know the birds are nesting because they come to the feeder in pairs and leave in pairs. Also, the females of the chickadees and titmice beg for food and the male feeds them—typical breeding behavior. My problem is compounded by the fact that there is no brushy undergrowth in the woods. When the birds leave they fly up into the top of the trees before heading back to their nests, and I lose sight of them very quickly. I should have better luck after their eggs hatch and they have four to six nestlings to feed. They won't be so circumspect then but will fly directly to the nest with food.

I have found some nests. The Carolina wrens have scorned all my nesting boxes and have built their nest in the top of a bag of cedar shavings saved for the dog's bed. This is the same spot they chose last year for their first brood, and the cat caught all the young before they left the nest. In spite of all I can do it will probably happen again this year. For their second brood they usually use one of the nesting boxes provided. They seem to be very fond of the open woodshed where I store the cedar chips, so I will put one of the boxes inside the woodshed for them.

A pair of blue jays are building a nest high up in a big beech tree near the back door. Usually very noisy birds, they are as silent as ghosts around their nest. A pair of bluebirds showed up in my garden last Friday and became interested in the nesting boxes. They were in and out of the box for about half an hour before the female decided she liked it and began to carry in nesting material.

Saturday evening I was sitting on the deck watching all this activity when I saw a wood duck fly along the edge of the woods and land in the fork of a big beech tree. Easing down through the woods, I found that the big tree has a large hollow in it, and I think the wood duck is nesting there. If she is, her ducklings are going to have a tough row to hoe when they hatch. First off, they will have to jump thirty feet to the ground; then, picking themselves up, they will have a fifty-yard hike to a big ditch, herded along by anxious parents; tumbling down into the ditch, they will have another mile to go before reaching a flooded swamp, where they will hopefully survive and grow up during the summer.

I put up my hummingbird feeder last week and had several hummingbirds buzzing around it before the morning was over. It will be a month or so before they start to think about nesting. I was fortunate last year and had three hummingbird nests around the edge of the yard.

The male great-crested flycatcher is back and busy calling and establishing a territory in the back yard. They nested in a box I provided for them last year, and I expect that they will nest there again when the females arrive in a couple of weeks.

8th May 1986

I have found the nests of the chickadees and titmice, but the nuthatches' nest continues to elude me. The great-crested fly-catchers are finally building a nest in the box they used last year; they refused to use it until I went up and patched a crack in it with roofing cement! The Carolina wrens, bluebirds, red-bellied woodpeckers, chickadees, titmice, mourning doves, and downy woodpeckers all now have young in the nests. A pair of blue jays are incubating eggs in their nest in the big beech tree in the yard. The summer tanager, wood thrush, wood-pewee, and Acadian flycatcher will all be building nests shortly. They scold me as I walk in the woods around the yard.

22nd May 1986

The Carolina wrens brought their six fledglings safely off the nest last week. That means I can let the cat out now without holding her hand! Next out of the nest will be the baby bluebirds from the nesting box in the garden. The white-breasted nut-hatches (whose nest I never did find) have brought three fledg-lings to the feeder, where they quiver and beg for food. They have adult plumage and look exactly like their parents.

The summer tanagers, whose nest is in the oak tree in the yard, hassled all afternoon on Thursday with a male scarlet tan-ager. The females of the two species are almost identical, and the male scarlet tanager was apparently interested in a closer ac-quaintance with the female summer tanager. The two males chased each other inconclusively all afternoon, and not until the female joined her mate was the male scarlet tanager finally routed.

A male prothonotary warbler showed up in the yard on May 12th and has been singing in the woods around the house ever since. He has not attracted a mate so far but it's not for lack of trying. I put out two gourd nesting boxes for him, and he is visiting both, sitting in the entrances and singing loudly. In this species it is the male who selects the nesting site. This is a beautiful golden little bird, the only cavity-nesting warbler in the east, and a treat for me to watch. They usually nest in swamps, so I hope he persists and finds a mate who will settle for a drier location and nest in one of the gourds so I can observe them more closely.

26th June 1986

On May 20 I found a ruby-throated hummingbird's nest by bee-lining* the female as she left my hummingbird feeder. She was still in the process of lining her nest with willow fluff, so I focused my Celestron telescope on it so I could observe more closely. The next day, as I was watching through the telescope, a female wood-pewee entered the field of view, hovered in front of the hummingbird nest, quickly plucked out a beakful of fluff, and flew off. I subsequently discovered that she was starting her nest on the dead limb of a maple tree about fifty yards from the hummingbird's nest. She returned for more material and was buzzed and driven off, bill snapping, by the returning female hummingbird. The pewee persisted, however, and during the day when the hummingbird was absent, she succeeded in totally destroying the hummingbird's nest. The hummingbird then abandoned that site and is now building in the woods on the other side of the house.

Two days later I saw the female pewee hovering above the almost completed nest of a pair of summer tanagers. As I watched she began to filch nest-lining material from this nest. She made several trips to the tanager nest during the day, taking substantial amounts of nest lining material from it. In the face of

---

* "Bee-lining" is a term lifted from the vocabulary of our pioneer ancestors when they were attempting to find a wild bee hive to rob for its honey. They would put out a bit of honey, and when wild bees found it and began to carry it back to their hive the hunter would observe the line of flight of the bees as they left the honey. Moving along this visual flight line, keeping the bees in sight, it was fairly easy to discover the hive. Using this technique it is easy to locate hummingbird nests, and I routinely discover three or four each year in the woods around the house.

this thievery the summer tanagers may have abandoned their nest site, as I haven't seen them around it for several days. The pewee must have watched both nests being built, as they were well concealed and hard to find. The pewee's nest is completed now, so presumably her neighbors' nests are safe. I had hoped to get good photographs of both the hummingbird and tanagers at their nests, so for a while I was so irritated at the pewee that I almost hoped that a sharp-shinned hawk would catch and eat her!

10th July 1986

I have about a dozen hummingbirds at my feeder, and the back yard around the feeder has turned into a battleground. The "top dog" for the last month is a one-eyed male. He is quite tame, but when I sit on the deck he always turns so his good eye is on my side. In the mornings and evenings when it's cool he sits right by the feeder and fights with almost every hummingbird who comes by. In the heat of the day he has a favorite perch up in the shade from which he dive-bombs visitors to "his" feeder. The interactions are interesting.

There are two other males who visit the feeder regularly. One of the two is allowed to drink his fill and depart in peace. The other is dive-bombed as soon as he appears, and the two perform spectacular acrobatics around the feeder before the intruder is driven away. Most of the females leave hurriedly when they hear the male diving out of the tree. One of them, however, is quite belligerent and persistent. They battle it out, and she usually gets to fill up at the feeder. She has a nest about a hundred yards back in the woods. I finally found it by bee-lining her as she left the feeder, then spending several hours on a stool back in the woods on her line of flight.

18th September 1986

Fall bird migration has started in earnest. Sunday morning a flock of a thousand or so grackles came filtering through the woods and across the back yard, scratching in the leaves and making a lot of noise. Fall warblers are passing through and, as usual, are difficult to identify correctly.

I stopped feeding the hummingbirds last week, and hopefully they are now winging their way across the Gulf of Mexico to their wintering ground in South America.

2nd October 1986

I don't fill my bird feeders during the summer, but it's getting time to overhaul them and get ready for another season. I prefer to mix my own bird seed using equal parts of black oil sunflower seed and white millet. Most birds won't eat the red millet, milo, wheat, etc. in the commercial mixes; it's cheap, just adds weight, and usually germinates or rots in the feeder. They all like sunflower seeds and white millet. I also put up a small separate thistle sock for goldfinches and pine siskins, and they will cling to it by the dozens. The brushpile near the main feeder has fallen pretty flat and needs to be replenished, and I need to rethink my anti-squirrel strategy.

A pair of pileated woodpeckers have decided to excavate a roosting hole in a big beech tree in the side yard, and in the mornings we get a good view of them from the bathroom window on the third floor as they pound away. They only work for about an hour each day so are apparently in no big hurry to finish the job. A big Cooper's hawk caught a grackle in the edge of the yard last week, and she is still hanging around in the woods.

6th November 1986

I'm having the same problem with my bird feeder this fall that I had last year: I'm back in the woods here and not near the edges of any fields, so birds are not finding my feeder. I'll have to do what I did last year—put up several feeders at the edge of the nearest field, and when birds start using them I'll leapfrog them, line of sight, up the driveway and back to the main feeder at the house. It works, but will take several weeks to accomplish.

The pair of pileated woodpeckers are still working on the hole they are excavating in the big beech tree in the side yard. They work for an hour or so each morning and have the hole in about four inches to date. It's probably going to be a roosting hole, not a nesting hole, but we'll see what happens there next spring.

11th December 1986

Birds are finally visiting my feeder in good numbers. Mostly they are juncos, white-throated sparrows, chickadees, nuthatches, tufted titmice, cardinals, and several red-bellied woodpeckers. An opportunistic male sharp-shinned hawk visits the feeder occasionally to see what he can catch. On Saturday he dashed across the driveway in front of the car in hot pursuit of a cardinal. I hope he didn't catch it, but he was only five feet behind and gaining when they both vanished at full speed into a large thicket of blackberry and grape vines.

The pair of pileated woodpeckers are progressing with their excavation of a roosting hole in the beech tree in the side yard. They work mostly at daybreak, but we see them busy at work sometimes when we return home from a day's outing. It's not deep enough to use yet, and they are investing so much time and effort in it that I have hopes that they may nest there in the spring.

1st January 1987

Activity around my feeder and in the yard has picked up considerably during the last week. On Sunday morning the side yard and garden area was full of palm warblers and bluebirds. The bluebirds were showing a lot of premature interest in the bluebird nesting boxes and the gourds put up for wrens and chickadees.

29th January 1987

Monday was such a miserable day that I turned my lounger to face the sliding glass doors and spent most of the day watching the birds at the feeder. My Christmas decorations on the door and around the lamp post included a lot of holly, so I took them down and put the branches with their red berries on a bench by the feeder. Bluebirds have been around the feeder for the last week, probably wondering why all the other birds were hanging around. They quickly found the holly berries and about ten of them were around for most of the day.

I was surprised to find that under artificial conditions (ie, at the feeder) they were quite aggressive towards each other and any other species that landed on the bench near the berries. On the feeder itself all the species, with the exception of the pine siskins, exhibited both intra-specific and extra-specific aggression, and the tray was the scene of constant conflict. This did not occur on the ground under the feeder, so I am assuming that each individual has a "personal space" around it and when this space is breached either fight or flight takes place.

(It's like the Englishman and the Arab who were introduced at a diplomatic function. Anglo Saxons in general feel uncomfortable conversing at distances of less than three feet, while Arabs in general feel uncomfortable conversing at distances of more than a foot and a half. Their ensuing conversation resembled a slow-motion dance, the Arab closing to his comfortable personal distance and the Englishman backing off to his comfortable personal distance, both feeling uncomfortable and neither knowing why!)

The cold weather and light snow brought in a lot of birds. There were white-throated sparrows, juncos, towhees, cardinals, purple finches, chickadees, white-breasted nuthatches, titmice, bluebirds, pine siskins, and a red-bellied woodpecker all active at the feeder tray. In addition there was a loud, un-sophisticated blue jay who had probably never seen a feeder before but was attracted by all the other birds.

12th February 1987

We will be having cold weather for a while yet, but the sun is getting a little higher in the sky each day, and nature is responding. I've seen several red-shouldered hawks putting on their spectacular courting flights, and horned owl duets are a nightly occurrence in the woods in back of the house. Several thousand grackles worked their way through the woods on Sunday and a lot of the males were strutting around, puffing out their feathers and giving their squeaky calls, not full courtship display yet but the blood is heating up.

26th February 1987

One of the questions I'm asked most often around town and among friends is: "What's happened to all the birds? My feeder is almost deserted this year."

The birds that come to our feeders are mostly seed eaters during the winter, and in spite of the very dry summer this was a very good year for grass and weed seeds. In the north, snow cover soon hides most of the seeds, and birds are forced to the feeders early on. Down here, seeds are readily available and birds stick with them until late in the winter when natural foods become scarce.

Here in the woods, my own feeder was slow to become fully utilized. First to come were the juncos and white-throated sparrows in November, then gradually other species began to show up. Starting in February my feeder began hosting hordes of birds. I have a dozen or so towhees who are around all day, twenty or thirty purple finches coming and going constantly, and flocks of pine siskins and goldfinches who stop by half a dozen times during the day. Small numbers of chickadees, nuthatches, and cardinals come and go, and last week a lone song sparrow showed up. Red-bellied woodpeckers who were common at the feeder last winter have yet to show up this winter.

My big plus this winter has been a flock of about fifteen evening grosbeaks. They show up at about 8 am, monopolize the feeder for half an hour, then are gone for several hours. They can really go through a bag of sunflower seed! Last week I noticed a brightly colored male evening grosbeak feeding among the leaves on the ground under a beech tree in the edge of the woods. I mounted the telephoto lens on my camera and left the house by a door on the opposite side of the house. By keeping tree trunks between myself and bird and moving very slowly (a half hour for sixty feet) and quietly, I was able to get within fifteen feet of it and get a series of color photographs. It was feeding on beech nuts which it found under the leaves, mashing the triangular nuts in its powerful beak to get at the kernel.

Several times a week birds will fly into my picture windows and stun themselves. I find that the best way to handle them is to pick them up quietly and gently and carefully place them in the bottom of a large paper grocery bag. I use the fold of the bag to close the top, and clip it shut with two clothespins. Then I place the bag in a warm, dark, quiet place, such as a closet. I leave it there for several hours, then quietly check it. If the bird appears alert I take it outside, lie the bag on its side pointing away from me and the house, open the top, and set the bird free. When I used to leave them alone on the deck about half of them died, apparently from concussion and exposure. The paper bag, dark, and warmth are crucial, because the bird becomes quiet, rests, and without additional stress has the best chance to recover. I haven't lost a bird since I adopted this method.

12th March 1987

We have some interesting activity going on in the side yard. For several months the pileated woodpeckers have been working on the two large beech trees about forty feet from the house. They enlarged an existing hole in each tree then proceeded to excavate a new hole just above the upper hole in the right-hand tree. At 8 AM on Wednesday morning last week I saw a pair of wood ducks sitting on a limb high up in one of the trees. After a minute the female flew down and began to investigate all four holes, even the unfinished one. After about twenty minutes she settled on the lower hole in the right-hand tree, entered it, and remained inside for twenty minutes. She then came out and flew off through the woods, followed by the male who had sat patiently nearby.

Suspecting that she might nest there, I removed the screen from the third-floor bathroom opposite the trees and installed a camouflage net over the window. Sure enough, at 8 AM the next day they were back and the female duplicated her activity, finally entering the lower hole and remaining inside for half an hour. As soon as the female emerged, both ducks flew off through the woods. I hoped the female was coming in each morning to lay an egg and would not start to incubate until the full clutch (eight to fifteen eggs) had been laid.

We watched at 8 AM on Thursday: nothing; at 8 AM on Friday: nothing; and at 8 AM on Saturday: nothing again. I figured that maybe she had just been checking out vacancies and had found something more attractive and secluded. Then, on Sunday at 6:30 AM I got up and looked out the window—and there she was, looking out of the hole. They may have decided to show up early on Thursday, Friday, and Saturday too, and left before we got up. This time she spent over an hour in the hole before they left.

The male always perches quietly nearby on watch, so we are having to rearrange our mornings to avoid alarming them: no lights turned on, no loud noises, no walking in front of windows, and no leaving the house until they have left. If they persist, we hope they will become used to us and we can resume normal activities but on a muted scale.

To add to the interest, the pileated woodpeckers are still working on the excavation just above the one the wood duck is in, and they peer in occasionally at the sitting female duck who hisses at them to make them leave. With any luck I may end up with a nesting wood duck in one hole and a nesting pileated woodpecker in the other, all in the same tree!

26th March 1987

The wood duck finally finished laying her clutch of eggs and began incubating them on March 17th. She sits in the nest hole in the beech tree and is calming down somewhat. We can leave via the back door now and even back the car around without flushing her off the nest. She leaves every morning at 6 AM for an hour of feeding and again at about 4 PM. The male flies shotgun when she returns but leaves as soon as she is settled. I have the Celestron telescope set up in a bedroom so we can check up on her during the day. She has a white ring around each eye, and in the dark hole that's about all we can see.

9th April 1987

It is still a little early for most birds to be nesting: the northern birds who spend the winter with us are mostly still here and our summer nesters who spend the winter in South America have not arrived back yet. I have located nesting pairs of about a dozen species, however, and the spring nesting season is about to burst upon us.

We are keeping a close watch on the incubating wood duck in the side yard. She has a week to ten days more before her eggs hatch.

23rd April 1987

9 AM, Monday, April 20th: The wood duck still has not brought off her brood. According to the information I've been able to gather, the incubation period for wood ducks is twenty-eight to thirty-one days. This female selected her nest site on March 2nd and for the next fourteen days spent about an hour each morning in the nest, presumably laying an egg each day, with the male waiting patiently in the tree outside the nest hole until she was ready to leave. On March 17th she stayed on the nest all day and we started timing her incubation from this date. She has stuck to this schedule ever since, only leaving for an hour or so each morning to feed. She has been on the nest for thirty-five days now—and still no ducklings.

I want to photograph the ducklings jumping from the tree to the ground, so I have been sitting near the window each day for the past week checking the nest at least once every hour through a powerful telescope. I can tell when she is inside because of her broad white eye-ring which shows up clearly back in the dark hollow, so I know she has been faithfully sitting on her eggs all day every day for the last thirty-five days. I hope something happens soon, because I'm getting cabin fever!

Being confined to the window or deck for the last week has forced me to observe activities in the woods around the yard more closely, and I have discovered the active nests of six species of birds in addition to the wood duck. The chickadees, nuthatches, mourning doves, and Carolina wrens all have young in the nests, and the red-bellied woodpeckers and the flickers are incubating eggs in theirs.

A male ruby-throated hummingbird showed up in the yard on April 14th. I got out my two feeders and put them both up, one in its old location by the deck and the small one on the lamppost. He found them both within twenty minutes and has taken up a perch where he can monitor both feeders and attempt to reserve them for his sole use. I can foresee a lively time when more males show up and when the females begin to arrive in a week or so.

9:45 AM: Hold everything! I take back everything I've been thinking about the wood duck. I just checked through the telescope and one little duckling was looking back at me from among its mother's breast feathers. It is covered with down, is a dark brown, and has light tan cheeks. It looked dry and active, so I'm going to get my camera set up to record them when they begin to leave the nest, hopefully some time today. I wish I had a little more sun but I'm now set up and ready so I'll continue with the journal while I'm waiting for the "coming-out party!"

I'm sitting in a makeshift blind at the window of the third-floor bathroom. With screen removed and the glass back I have an excellent view both of the wood duck nest and of the deciduous woods behind it. The trees are leafing out and rapidly fleshing out the bare bones of the trees. In a week or so it will be one big green wall, but for now I can see quite a ways into it. A flush of spring Warblers are moving through it this morning, calling continuously, and while watching them with binoculars I picked up a slight movement and have been able to locate seven deer, all bedded down and chewing their cud. We see this group around the house almost every day. The other night fourteen were standing in the driveway when we left the house.

9:40 AM, Tuesday, April 21st: The wood ducks just came off! I have been watching since dawn. The mother came out shortly several times, flew around briefly, then returned. At 9.35 she flew down to the ground below the nest. She must have called softly, because all the little ducklings lined up at the entrance and jumped in a long line, just like paratroopers coming out of a plane. There were eleven of them altogether, and most of them were in the air at the same time. They were all down in less than five seconds.

Ducklings do a considerable amount of soft peeping from within the shell before they hatch, and the mother talks back to them. When they hatch and as they dry out, they and the mother continuously vocalize together. It is this process which bonds the young to their mother so they will recognize her, follow her closely, and instantly obey her summons and commands. It takes a lot of bonding to make a tiny duckling obey his mother's call and unhesitatingly take the forty-foot jump from the nest to the ground.

The mother crouched low and led them through the may-apples and leaves back to the big ditch in the edge of the woods. The ducklings stayed so close to her and she crouched so low that they looked like some strange kind of animal snaking through the may-apple plants!

2nd July 1987

Sunday evening was very still, not a leaf stirring, and I sat on the back deck from 8 PM until dark at about 9:15 PM. A pair of summer tanagers scolded from the edge of the yard until almost dark; they have a nest in the edge of the woods.

There was a lot of activity around the hummingbird feeder from 8 PM until about 8:45 PM. Because of their high metabolism, hummingbirds have to really stock up with food for the night. In addition, they become torpid during the night to further conserve energy. I have about eight at the feeder, and they were buzzing and squabbling, each trying to take on about a third of their body weight in sugar water. In addition to fighting among themselves, they have been going around and around with bumblebees at the feeder during the day, so much so that I have taken the fly swatter to the bees, clearing out at least half a dozen a day.

16th July 1987

A pair of bluebirds are building a nest in my garden—or perhaps I should say that the female bluebird is building the nest: the male flies alongside and sings pretty, but that's all! This is the second brood in that box this year, and if fledged successfully it will be the fifth brood raised in my boxes this year.

Activity around my feeder has dropped off considerably, but I have rigged up a drip-type bird bath in the side yard that is proving to be very popular with several species of woodland birds. A pair of wood-pewees in particular are spending a lot of time around it.

30th July 1987

For the past month or so I haven't been paying too much attention to the big bird feeder in the back yard. On Saturday I cleaned it out and dumped a dipperful of sunflower seeds in the tray. While I was at it I mixed a recipe of peanut butter, yellow cornmeal, hog lard, and flour, and filled my two hole-type feeders

RUBY-THROATED HUMMINGBIRD
Archilochus colubris

with this mixture. Red-bellied woodpeckers, cardinals, titmice, and chickadees are becoming active at the seed feeder, and the titmice and chickadees at the peanut mixture also.

Last night about dusk a barred owl came gliding through the woods and lit in a tree near the feeders. It sat there for half and hour, silently scanning the ground and nearby trees for prey. Several wood thrushes saw it land, and flitted around in the undergrowth scolding it vigorously for ten minutes or so before slipping away to roost for the night.

10th September 1987

There are a lot of hummingbirds migrating through just now and very busy at my feeders, which I have filled for the last time this year. As soon as they are empty I'll clean them and put them away till next spring. This is so the hummingbirds won't be tempted to stay here too long and will get on with their migration to South America.

A few wood warblers are starting to come through the woods on their fall migration. Black-throated blue, black-throated green, and American redstarts were all around the yard on Friday. In spite of the squares of red paper taped to the glass doors and windows, a few birds fly into them and some are killed. I picked up an ovenbird and a wood-pewee this morning, and caught and released from the greenhouse a male black-throated blue warbler and two hummingbirds.

24th September 1987

A barred owl has been hanging around the yard for the past several weeks. It is active during the day, and from observations I think that it is catching skinks in the yard and garden. The squirrels and birds make a lot of fuss whenever it appears, but I have not seen it make any attempt to catch one. It's around at night too, making a lot of spooky moans and screams. I hope it doesn't catch any of the flying squirrels who are coming to the feeder for peanut butter every evening.

A few kestrels have arrived from the north and are hunting mice and grasshoppers from the power line; they will eat a lot of them. Warblers continue to pass through the woods, the most numerous being redstarts. They are probably the most beautiful of our wood warblers and are quite tame.

29th October 1987

Our oldest son, Pepper, and his family spent three days with us last week. In addition to being an excellent naturalist he is a professional ornithologist, so we had plenty to look at and talk about.

Wintering swamp and song sparrows have arrived in large numbers and could be readily spished* out into the open for observation. The first juncos have showed up at the feeder, and it won't be long before mixed flocks of juncos and white-throated sparrows will descend on us. The big brushpile that I have by the feeder as cover for the birds has virtually collapsed, so I'm going to have to rebuild it if I want to keep birds around the feeder.

The barred owl who has been hanging around the yard all summer showed up on Monday with the most unowl-like behavior. It landed on a stump in the sun, spread its wings and tail, and sunbathed for a half hour or so. Small birds fussed around it and squirrels scolded it continuously, but it ignored them all. That night when I went out to my shop, it flew from a stump near the walk and hooted continuously as it flew down the driveway. It is a weird owl!

19th November 1987

On Saturday and Sunday morning we were swamped with grackles and robins. The grackles were feeding on beech nuts

---

* "Spishing" is the sound made by pursing one's lips and making a hissing sound. It resembles the scolding notes of birds when they are attempting to drive away predators. Birds come to a person making this sound to help scold, so it is an excellent way to get them in close.

in the trees around the yard, and there must have been about ten thousand of them. They made a tremendous din as they foraged in the trees and among the fallen leaves. When I clapped my hands together sharply there was a sudden silence, followed by a loud roar as they all took flight; the noise resumed as they circled around and landed again. The robins are early fall migrants who are feeding on dogwood berries. They will hang around in bands of forty or fifty until they have eaten all the berries, then they will move on.

The shorter days and cooler weather have apparently energized the pileated woodpeckers and flickers. They spend an hour or so every morning excavating material from their roosting holes in three big beech trees around the yard. I keep hoping that the pileateds will nest here one spring.

10th December 1987

Horned owls are about ready to nest, and a pair of them (bass and tenor) called most of Sunday night from the woods around the house. They were still around on Monday and were discovered by a flock of crows who harassed them for most of the morning. I'll keep an eye open for them while the leaves are off the trees.

24th December 1987

Nothing new has shown up at the feeder for the past several weeks. I have lots of titmice, chickadees, nuthatches, juncos, towhees, and white-throated sparrows. Several red-bellied woodpeckers are steady customers, and half a dozen cardinals slip in at about dusk and stoke up on sunflower seeds before going to roost. Carolina wrens, who couldn't care less about seeds, have discovered the peanut butter mixture I've put out and have developed quite a taste for it.

Surprisingly, blue jays, who nest in the yard during the summer, apparently leave the woods for civilization during the winter and have not discovered the feeder. A sharp-shinned hawk has, however, and several times this week has sent small birds diving into the brushpile or, if they are too far from cover, to freeze motionless where they sit; looking at them through binoculars I can't even see them blink. They have a very short memory, or—perhaps—out of sight out of mind, for within a minute of the hawk's leaving they are carrying on as usual.

7th January 1988

A few purple finches are showing up now, along with pine siskins and goldfinches. Several of the goldfinch males are showing a lot of yellow for this early in the year.

21st January 1988

I have four fox sparrows at my feeder now, and since they are such beautiful birds I decided on Sunday morning to get close-up photographs of them. I draped camouflage cloth over a table on the deck, crawled under it, and lay flat, resting the camera on a bean-bag. It worked fine. In about twenty minutes I got photographs of fox sparrows, white-throated sparrows, and juncos. However, when it came time to get to my knees and back out from under the table I almost couldn't make it. My mind is as young as ever but I guess my muscles and backbones are getting old!

3rd March 1988

We are awakened every morning now by a whole series of *rat-a-tats* as four species of woodpecker stake out their territories in the woods around the house. They each select a dry hollow tree or branch that will resonate well and drum on it with their beaks in a series of one- or two-second bursts. In order of volume they go from the tapping of the little downy woodpecker, through the red-bellied and flicker, to the booming of the big pileated. It's interesting that all four species will share the same territory but none of them will tolerate another pair of the same species as themselves in the common territory.

It's the same with bluebirds. If two boxes are in sight of one another, they have to be about a hundred yards apart in order to have two pairs nesting. In the north, where bluebirds are not very common and have a lot of competition from house sparrows, we put two bluebird houses about twenty yards apart. A tree swallow would take one box and, hopefully, a bluebird the other. The tree swallow didn't seem to mind the bluebird and would help drive the house sparrows out of the area.

17th March 1988

Lots of activity around the yard last week.

First of all the wood ducks showed up. The female investigated all of the pileated woodpecker holes in the two beech trees in the side yard and seemed to settle on the hole they used last year. However, the pileated woodpeckers have been doing a lot of work in both trees and the female duck doesn't appear to be comfortable with their presence. The ducks left and stayed away for several days, then showed up again and went through the entire routine again. They left after about an hour, showed up the next morning, and this time looked over holes and hollows in a lot of different trees in the woods around the house. I had put up a box for them on a tree in back of my workshop but a squirrel took it over and chased the ducks away when they investigated it. As soon as they left I acquired another wood duck box and quickly put it up back in the woods. We haven't seen the pair back for several days, so maybe they found a suitable hole or hollow somewhere else.

While this was going on, a different kind of activity was taking place near the back door. There is a beech stump there, about three feet tall and ten inches in diameter, and it has apparently reached the proper stage of decay. A chickadee thinks so, anyway, and last week started to excavate a nest hole in the south side near the top. The pair have been working steadily all week and just about have it finished. We have had to keep the cat in the house unless we are watching her, because she can reach the hole by standing on her hind legs. If the chickadees persist and begin to line the nest cavity with deer hair and feathers I will build a chicken-wire fence around the stump to keep the cat away.

I have another box on a tree near the stump. I put this up last fall, hoping to get a prothonotary warbler to nest this spring. During the winter deermice found it and build a nest in it. Last week a pair of white-breasted nuthatches decided to take it over. They proceeded to demolish and toss out the deermouse nest and build their own in its place. I don't know why they went to the trouble of tossing out the mouse nest, as they are putting the same kind of material back in for their own nest!

31st March 1988

The wood ducks showed up again and finally made up their minds. They decided on the nest site that they used last year, and the female has been laying eggs in it for a week or so. Last Sunday she stayed all day and began incubation. We'll see how many days it takes this year. The pileated woodpeckers peek in at her occasionally but have given up trying to roost in that tree.

The chickadees are lining their nest cavity in the stump in the back yard so I have erected a fence to keep the cat away. The deermice in the nest box successfully resisted eviction by the white-breasted nuthatches, who then selected an empty nest box near the driveway. They are very energetic and fun to watch. Both birds worked on the nest initially, then the female stayed inside and the male passed nesting material in to her. I watched him bring leaves and pine needles, which he just dumped into the nest hole. He also visits the feeder and brings shucked sunflower seeds to the female; he lands by the hold and calls, and the female sticks her head out and takes the seed.

The red-bellied woodpeckers are excavating a new nest hole lower down in the same dead hornbeam tree they used last year. Early on sunny mornings the woods around the house resound with the territorial drummings of the four different woodpecker species, and during the rest of the day the quieter, slower tempo of nest excavation can be heard.

The juncos and white-throated sparrows are still at the feeder, but the white-throated males are giving their spring calls; one morning soon I'll look out and they will be gone. A few of the goldfinch males have gotten their dandelion yellow and will soon be gone too. The chickadees, cardinals, titmice, nuthatches, and towhees will be with me year round, so the feeder will keep busy. The word appears to be getting around among the flying squirrels. I looked out the other night and there were six of them at the feeder. They sure eat a lot of the peanut butter mixture!

5th May 1988

It has been a very interesting two weeks in our back yard.

Remember the white-breasted nuthatches who built a nest in one of the nesting boxes near the house? On the morning of April 14th the male appeared to be very agitated, flying from tree trunks close by to the nest box, running all over it, peering in the nest hole, then flying back to nearby tree trunks, all the while calling loudly. I assumed that the eggs had hatched and that the new father didn't know what to make of the nestlings. Hatching was confirmed shortly when the female appeared with food and carried it into the nest box. During the absence of the pair, I looked into the nest. There were six nestlings, about two to three days old, nestled deep in a well-made nest of bark, moss, hair, and fine vegetable fibers. The male made no attempt to feed the young. He followed the female on her foraging trips, calling constantly. He would peer into but would not enter the box. The male continued this behavior for the rest of the day.

I was away during the following morning and resumed my observations early in the afternoon. The female continued to forage and feed the young, while the male, still very agitated and vocal, followed her on about half of these foraging trips. He spent the balance of the time around the nest site. Now, however, when the female was absent, he entered the nest cavity and emerged with his beak full of nesting material. Some of this he "caulked" into cracks and crevices on the outside of the nest box, some he caulked into bark crevices, and some he simply tossed out. He ceased this activity when the female arrived, and would not enter the nest box while she was inside or nearby. The female made no attempt to interfere, and continued to feed the nestlings. About 6 PM, in the absence of both parents, I opened the nest box to check the young. About half of the nest material had been removed. The nestlings were pretty exposed but appeared to be okay. The weather was in the seventies, and the female did not linger in the nest to brood the nestlings when she brought food.

The temperature dropped to 40 degrees during the night and stood at 44 degrees when I resumed operations the next morning. The male was on the outside of the box, very agitated and vocal, and the female appeared almost immediately carrying food and entered the box. She stayed inside for six minutes, appeared at the entrance for a few minutes looking flustered, then went back in for another four minutes. As soon as she left, the male entered the nest and began to toss out nest material. I opened the nest box and found almost all of the nest material was gone. The nestlings were huddled on a few small wood chips and nest detritus in the bottom of the box; they were cold to the touch and all were violently shivering. I took some down spilled from the wood-duck nest, covered the nestlings with it, and also put back into the box some of the nesting material that the male had tossed out. The female returned, spent ten minutes inside, then left. I quickly checked again and found that she had rearranged the down and nesting material around the nestlings and had apparently brooded them for a short time. As soon as I left the nest site, the male immediately entered the nest cavity and began to toss out nesting material. At this point, concerned about the survival of the nestlings, I removed the male.

My thinking is that this male is not the original male of the pair: something must have happened to the original male quite recently and a new male showed up and filled the vacancy. The new male was destroying the nest in an attempt to force the female to re-nest so he could father the next brood. This kind of activity is apparently quite common with some of the primates, rhesus and langur monkeys for example, where a new alpha male will kill all the very young in the troop when he takes over. When their young are killed, the females involved go into estrus in a short time and the new male then breeds with them, insuring that all the young will soon be carrying his genes. There is some indication that this might happen with birds also. I think that activity like this has been reported for house wrens and perhaps acorn woodpeckers. In these instances, however, it has been eggs that were destroyed by the new male.

As far as I can tell, this activity has never been observed with nuthatches, and never with any species of bird after the eggs have hatched. Nuthatches are single-brooded, and I doubt that a female would re-nest after so much time and energy had been expended, even if the first attempt was unsuccessful. In this case, the hardworking female has raised them all successfully. All six of them fledged early Sunday and she led them back into the woods.

The wood duck nesting in the beech trees in the side yard hatched her eggs on the morning of April 27th. We kept an eye on her during the day, but she kept the ducklings in the nest the first day and night as she did last year. The next morning I set up my camera around 8 AM and we kept watch. We could see the ducklings moving around inside. At 9:30 AM the female began to peer out of the hole, looking carefully all around and up into the sky. She repeated this several times, then at 10 AM she flew down to the ground below the nest and began to call immediately. Three little ducklings jumped at once and hurried to her. She continued to call, and six more appeared in the entrance and jumped. A stiff breeze was blowing, and these six landed about ten feet from her. When the ducklings hit the ground at the end of the forty-foot drop they each bounced about a foot. The mother quickly gathered them all about her and led them to a nearby ditch. This leads to a flooded area back in the woods and it's there that she will raise them.

The chickadees by the back door will be fledging in a day or so, followed by the titmice in the back yard, then the bluebirds in the garden. Then, this morning I watched a hummingbird start to build a nest over the driveway. There's always something going on around here!

19th May 1988

Hummingbirds are very scarce at my feeder this year. The most I've seen at any one time have been two. The female who built the nest along my driveway had bad luck: during a storm a dead limb fell from the tree overhead, hit the small branch the nest was attached to, and bounced out both the eggs. I found them on the ground under the nest, about the size of navy beans and both cracked. I've watched the nest for a week and the female has not returned. She will probably not re-nest this year.

I cleaned out the nest box that the nuthatch had raised her brood in, and a pair of great-crested flycatchers have begun to build a nest in it. The wood thrush nesting near the garden has hatched her eggs and is busy foraging in the yard and garden for insects, mostly crickets, to feed her young. I suspect that she is raising cowbirds as well as her own, and I will check the nest in a day or so.

23rd June 1988

The hummingbird with the nest in the side yard fledged two young last Saturday. A Carolina wren with a nest under the boat seat on the deck hatched her eggs on Saturday morning, and if we can keep the cat away the young should fledge in about two weeks. The bluebirds in the garden have started to build a nest for their second brood there this year.

7th July 1988

Until recently I thought that hummingbirds only raised one brood each year; I think I'm going to have to change my mind. I watched one female hummingbird raise a brood in a beech tree near the deck; the young fledged on June 20th. This week I noticed a female hummingbird building a nest in a beech tree near my workshop, and I suspect that this is a second brood, which will fledge sometime in August. I guess if you keep your eyes open you'll learn new things every day.

28th July 1988

Right now birds seem more interested in water than in my bird feeders. I have several large pottery saucers with water in them scattered around the yard, and the birds—particularly titmice and chickadees—come in family groups to take baths.

In addition, I have a small section of garden with fine, dry, sandy soil. In the late morning and early afternoon it is in full sun and the soil gets quite hot. Flickers, crested flycatchers, wood thrushes, and blue-gray gnatcatchers are in it constantly taking dust baths. They fly down, spread their wings and tails, fluff up the rest of their feathers, and grovel around in the dust like little wind-up toys, before finally freezing, head up, mouth open. They sit there in a trance for several minutes and only leave when it gets too hot to stand any longer. I guess the hot dust either kills or discourages mites. There is lots of cover in the garden, so I am rigging up a drip water bath for them there as well.

15th September 1988

Fall migration is in full swing, and while sitting on the deck Monday morning I observed several black-throated blue warblers, three black-and-white warblers, and an American redstart, all working the edges of the woods.

10th November 1988

So far this year I have seen a few juncos and heard the plaintive whistle of white-throated sparrows from hedgerows but I have very little activity at my feeder. The chickadees, nuthatches, and titmice that were here all summer and early fall have disappeared, and the sunflower seed in my feeder is sprouting! I always flush a few palm warblers from the grass along my driveway, but these odd little warblers won't come back into the woods. They spend the winter in the fields and corn stubble.

1st December 1988

The leaves are all gone from most of the trees in the woods around the house, and the sparrows and juncos are venturing into my feeders. I remade the big brushpile near the feeder so that feeder birds will have cover for protection. A good thing too, because a sharp-shinned hawk landed on a deck-railing post Saturday morning and sat for about five minutes, watching for breakfast. All the feeder birds wisely stayed motionless in the brushpile until it left.

A barred owl is hanging around, coming into the yard about 4 PM most evenings. It doesn't appear to be interested in the feeder birds but watches the gray squirrels intently. Flickers and pileated woodpeckers, who are going to roost at about this time, make a lot of fuss whenever it appears. It is getting used to us and is quite tame.

15th December 1988

Sunday afternoon I turned the recliner around to face the sliding glass doors, the bird feeder, and the woods beyond, and sat back with a pair of binoculars and took an afternoon census of the birds at my feeder.

The birds come and go, but at present I figure I have two song sparrows, twenty white-throated sparrows, two dozen juncos, ten titmice, eight chickadees, five nuthatches, one hairy wood-pecker, two downy woodpeckers, two red-bellied woodpeckers, and one Carolina wren. Two pileated woodpeckers and several flickers were busy around the yard. They roost in two hollow beech trees in the side yard but do not come to the feeder. I also have at least six fat gray squirrels and I'm going to have to figure out a way to keep them from actually sitting in the feeder. The two red-bellied woodpeckers are in the process of settling who's boss, and several times they fluttered to the ground locked in combat.

During the afternoon one of the nuthatches flew into the win-dow, in spite of pasted cut-outs, and stunned itself. Its mate flew down beside it and called agitatedly, but it just sat there gasping. It was cold, so after a while I picked it up, put it in a large paper bag, and put it in a warm dark closet to recover. After an hour or so it began to flutter in the bag, so I took it out to release it. It clung to my hand and climbed up my arm but would not fly. It probably has concussion, so I put it back in the closet and will try to release it in the morning.

I was surprised that I did not see any cardinals today; they are usually the last birds at the feeder before dark. The white-throated sparrows stayed around until 5 PM, by which time it had become too dark to make them out. Actually, my feeder is too far into the woods to attract a wide variety of birds because birds are mostly creatures of edges.

9th February 1989

A red-bellied woodpecker has been working for several weeks excavating either a nesting hole or a roosting hole in a large limb of a maple near the yard. It already has the hole deep enough for it to disappear inside.

2nd March 1989

Nothing seems to concentrate birds as much as a heavy snowfall. If they have been coming to a feeder they will show up in droves after a snowstorm and stay all day. If they are not used to a feeder they will look for areas of thin snow or areas where the snow has melted. I spent last Sunday photographing birds and had the best of both worlds. My feeder was swamped.

I didn't have that many new species but the numbers were tripled. I had purple finches, towhees, juncos, song sparrows, white-throated sparrows, fox sparrows, chickadees, titmice, Carolina wrens, downy and hairy woodpeckers, white-breasted nuthatches, brown creepers, red-bellied woodpeckers, goldfinches and blue jays. Around the yard but not at the feeder were pileated woodpeckers, flickers, bluebirds, and robins. In the field beside my driveway there was a flock of about a hundred pipits; I tried to get photographs of them, but they stayed out in the corn stubble.

30th March 1989

The wood duck pair showed up in the two big beech trees in the side yard last week. They spent an hour or so investigating the four holes in the beeches then flew off. Two days later they came back and repeated the process, on this occasion spending more time in the hole they used last year. In another two days they returned again. This time the hen flew directly into the hole and could be seen inside turning and twisting, shaping the nest. For the last couple of mornings they have come in at 7 AM. The hen goes directly into the nest and remains inside for about a half hour. The male perches on a nearby limb and keeps watch. When the hen leaves the nest she flies quickly through the woods, and the male follows closely. These are egg-laying trips now, and we think that there are six eggs in the nest already. (Last year she hatched nine ducklings, and the year before that, eleven.)

The white-breasted nuthatches are nest building in a nesting box in the front yard. I was curious as to why they were not using the nest box they used last year until I saw a flying squirrel sticking its head out of the entrance. The male nuthatch persistently performs an activity known as "bill-wiping" around the nest entrance: holding something dark in his bill, he wipes his bill sideways around the entrance and over the front of the nest box. Through the telescope it looked as if he had a carpenter ant or a black beetle of some kind in his bill and was rubbing it against the wood. Carpenter ants emit formic acid and several beetle species emit chemicals with disagreeable odors, and the nuthatch may be smearing these chemicals around the entrance to discourage deermice and flying squirrels who may attempt to take over the nest hole. As far as I know, biologists are still undecided about the significance of this behavior. A related species, the red-breasted nuthatch, smears pine pitch around the entrance to its nest, apparently to discourage competitors.

20th April 1989

My first hummingbird of the spring showed up on April 5th. It was a male in full spring courting plumage. He spent a half hour or so among the red columbine flowers in the wildflower garden and then took off down the driveway. He–or another male– showed up the next day, also spent time among the columbines, then left. I put up the hummingbird feeder but haven't noticed any customers yet. I suspect that these early hummingbird males are ones who have the farthest to go, up along the Canadian border, and that our resident ones will be along a week or so later.

The males always arrive first, set up a territory from which they exclude other males, and await the arrivals of the females. The females select a desirable territory and are courted by, and eventually mate with, the resident male. As far as I could determine, last year the male who had his territory centered on my back yard had six females in residence. The females get no help from the male in building the nest or in raising the young. The male's sole job is apparently to be strong, alert, and aggressive and to pass along the genes for these traits to his offspring.

I had a small cattail marsh on my farm in New York State, and it always amused me each spring when the male red-winged blackbirds arrived to set up their territories. They fought one another for weeks, sorting out and establishing territories. They were so full of aggression that even when the females arrived and settled in their territories several weeks later, they attempted to drive them out also. The females, determined to nest and raise their young in such a desirable habitat, were forced to dodge and hide in the cattails for a week or so until the males finally came to their senses and saw them as objects of desire, not competitors to be evicted!

On Tuesday morning I shared the surprise of many here in Chowan County who looked out their windows to find four inches of snow on the ground. Back in the woods out my way, tree limbs were breaking with cracks like rifle shots. The early hummingbirds are going to have a hard time for a day or so, and many of them may not survive. I brushed the snow off the hummingbird feeder, and hope that some of these early migrants will find their way to it. This snow is going to be hard on all the birds. Along with the early hummingbirds, the early warbler migrants will be hard put to survive unless the snow melts very quickly. For the others, don't put your feeders away yet, and please get those hummingbird feeders out as soon as possible. Our feathered friends will love you for it.

4th May 1989

We have been keeping a close eye on the wood duck nest in the beech tree in the side yard. She had been sitting on the eggs for a full month by April 30th. She appeared very restless on Saturday, turning and twisting and changing position, but we could not see any ducklings. At about 7 o'clock the next morning, while Dorothy was checking out the nest through binoculars, a small head popped up, and we knew that the brood had hatched.

The mother became increasingly restless, looking out of the nest hole and examining the ground below the nest and around the yard. When she stood up we could see a lot of little ducklings underfoot, and one even climbed on her back. From her actions I realized she was going to bring them out within a few minutes. She squeezed out of the nest hole and flew down to the ground at the base of the tree. She walked around the tree trunk then called. The ducklings crowded into the entrance hole and began to jump one at a time, to the ground forty feet below. There were thirteen of them this year, and the last three jumped together. They bounced on the wet honeysuckle and were quickly called together by the mother. When she had gathered them all, she led them through the may-apples and atamasco lilies to a water-filled ditch. The ducklings jumped into the water after the mother, and the whole flotilla swam down the ditch and back into the flooded woods.

I have been enjoying the hummingbirds' courting antics for the past week and several days ago started bee-lining the females as they left the feeders. I have three lines of flight plotted now, and on Monday morning I located a female building a nest along one of them. She is fairly close to my back door. I set up the Celestron telescope and have been watching her bring in lichens and spider silk to form the nest. First she wrapped lichens and the spider silk around a small branch then proceeded to make a small platform on top of it. She brings in small pieces of lichens, sits on the platform, and is beginning to build a form-fitting nest around her. I hope nothing interrupts her, as I would like to watch the entire nest-building and later, when she is raising her young, take some more photographs.

15th June 1989

I spent several hours Sunday afternoon sitting in a canvas chair in my driveway with a good view of one of my hummingbird feeders. I'm pretty sure now that in addition to the two known nests I have three additional nests in the trees close to the yard.

While sitting quietly and watching, I also found the nest of an ovenbird. It is on the ground, hidden among the leaves, and has four brown-spotted white eggs in it. I'll take photographs later when the eggs hatch, taking care not to get too close and disturb the parents. This is only the third ovenbird nest I've ever seen.

I also observed a pair of Acadian flycatchers building a nest in the back yard. This is the only *Empidonax* species nesting in the south. I think this is the same pair I've been observing, and if it is, then this is the third nest I've watched them build this spring. I hope they lay a clutch of eggs in this one and get on with the business of raising a brood!

6th July 1989

The trees around the south and west side of our house are growing and arching over the deck, making it a much more cool and shady retreat these hot, muggy, afternoons, and I spend considerable time there, camera and binoculars at hand.

Three baby Acadian flycatchers fledged Sunday evening from the nest at the edge of the yard and are begging and practicing flying around the edges of the yard today. There seems to be only one parent in attendance, and he or she has taken exception to the cat, who sleeps on the deck or on the base of my porpoise sculpture, and scolds her vigorously. The hummingbirds are very actively fussing around both feeders, and one of the nests has fledged two young.

The ovenbird nest back in the woods has been raided, and all four eggs are gone. After I discovered it I had purposely stayed well away from it. Foxes, raccoons, dogs, and other predators will often follow a human trail through the woods out of curiosity, and I didn't want to lead anything to the nest. This has been a very hard year in my woods for nesting birds. About seventy-five percent of all the nests I have observed being built this year were destroyed before the young could fledge. Most of the predators around my yard this year were crows, and I'm strongly tempted to part the hair of half a dozen or so with a 22!

20th July 1989

The male bluebird who has been raising a second brood in the box in the garden spent most of the morning last Saturday flying around the box calling persuasively, trying to get the nestlings to come out. As a matter of fact, he was so vocal that I thought something was wrong and opened the door to check. There was only one nestling in the box and it was okay so I closed the box, and by mid afternoon the parent had coaxed it out. It flew surprisingly well, and the two spent the rest of the day in the garden and yard. They were gone in the morning, so I cleaned out the box in case the male finds a mate and they decide to raise a third brood this year.

The hummingbird babies are out and flying well. They have inherited in full measure all of the rugged individualism and orneryness of the species, and all I have to do to get involved in their squabbles is to sit close to the feeders or the monarda bed. They soon accept my presence and zoom and chase one another around my chair. I'm getting so many hummers now that I think some of them are early migrants working their way south to the Gulf of Mexico and eventually the flight across it to South America. They are at the feeder until very late.

Saturday evening I sat out 'til dusk watching half a dozen pipistrelle bats that were hunting among the tops of the tall trees around the yard. Hummingbirds were still coming to the feeder, and to my surprise a pair of Acadian flycatchers were hawking insects among the tree tops. These little birds nest in the deep woods where the light is fairly dim during the day, so their eyesight is adapted to hunting in poor light. These appeared to be hunting insects happily up among the bats.

21st September 1989

A few hummingbirds are still passing through, and I'll leave the feeders up until the end of the month, but the main push has passed through. Fall warblers are passing through the woods each day, a kestrel has taken up its fall and winter station on the power lines along my driveway, and last Friday a magnificent peregrine falcon flew low overhead as I walked up the fifth fairway at the Chowan Golf and Country Club.

5th October 1989

It's about time to get my bird feeders ready for a new season. I put the last of my old sunflower and millet seed out last week, and the chickadees, nuthatches, titmice, cardinals, and blue jays soon cleaned it up. It will be a month or so before we get our wintering sparrows and finches, but it's best to have everything ready and avoid a last-minute rush.

9th November 1989

Around this area we never see the big numbers of bird migrants, but juncos, swamp sparrows, and phoebes are here for the winter, and last Friday I heard the lovely whistle of white-throated sparrows and saw a dozen or so. Kestrels have taken up winter territories on telephone wires out this way, and several marsh hawks are coursing low over the fields and ditches.

7th December 1989

Birds are becoming quite active at my feeder now that I've built up my brushpile. Of winter birds I have juncos, song sparrows, white-throated sparrows, and on Sunday an early fox sparrow showed up. The towhees who spend the summer in the pine plantation near our house are visiting the feeder regularly again.

A couple of phoebes are not interested in the feeder but are hanging around the yard catching chilled flies and wagging their tails. One warm evening at dusk last week as I stood on the deck watching bats hunting over the yard, five woodcock in a tight little group came flying over my head and dropped down among the trees just beyond the yard. This is the first time I have ever seen more than two together. They are nocturnal and will probably winter among the leaves in my woods.

18th January 1990

I have a lot of fox sparrows at my feeder, and goldfinches and purple finches are showing up in numbers now. During the snowstorm and the week following I put out about a hundred pounds of seed. A yellow-bellied sapsucker is eating all the berries from my holly wreaths and lamppost bouquets, and the Crowells have one who is visiting their seed feeder.

8th February 1990

It's time again to clean out the bluebird nest boxes; my bluebirds have been calling around the yard for the past several days. Three of the boxes I've put up for bluebirds around the edges of the yard have been taken over by flying squirrels, but there are still three left for the bluebirds in the garden, which is too open for the squirrels' tastes.

1st March 1990

I was a little optimistic when I said that three of my seven bluebird boxes had been taken over by flying squirrels; actually five of them contain flying squirrels. I constructed three more Bluebird nest boxes and put them up in areas a little farther from trees, where the flying squirrels won't be so strongly tempted to take over.

15th March 1990

The wood ducks showed up at the hollow beech tree in the side yard on February 21st. This same pair has nested there for the last three years, and this is the earliest they have shown up. They were here regularly for about half an hour every morning for the next ten days. Then on March 4th the female stayed in the nest hole for about an hour and could be seen twisting and turning. She has repeated this performance ever morning for the last seven days, so I think she has seven eggs laid so far. The male arrives with her and patiently waits on a nearby limb until she is ready to leave. When she has her clutch laid she will start to stay all day on the nest, and the male will cease to hang around.

Some other interesting activity has been going on in our side yard this last week. One of the bluebird nest boxes that I put up was taken over last year by a pair of white-breasted nuthatches who raised a brood in it. When they left, flying squirrels moved in and have been there all winter. About a week ago the nuthatches became interested in the nest box again and began crawling over the box, peering inside, and calling and thumping the box. This was apparently too much for the squirrels, who have left, and the nuthatches have moved in. The female remains inside and the male brings nesting material which he passes in to the female, who makes the nest to suit herself.

Saturday evening I observed both birds engaged in bill-wiping. Each bird had a dark substance in its bill and they were both walking all over the nest box, wiping the substance energetically over the box and the tree trunk the box was on. I slowly eased closer to the nest box, and when the female momentarily caulked her wiping material in a crack on the outside of the box, I rushed up and collected it before she could retrieve it. It is an odd substance—could be some species of jelly fungus or perhaps a mashed up insect larva. As far as I know, no one has ever collected any of the material the nuthatches use. I'm sending this to David Lee at the North Carolina Museum of Natural Sciences. I figure that David will have access to the proper "-ologist" to get it identified. I really want to know what the material is so that I can figure our what the nuthatches are doing and why they are doing it. The more you watch, the curiouser things become!

29th March 1990

The wood duck in the hollow beech tree in the side yard is about halfway through her incubation. She leaves twice a day to feed, and the male escorts her back to the nest. The nuthatches and bluebirds have selected nest boxes and are both incubating, but our migrating summer birds have not arrived yet. I did see several purple martins this week, so the rest should be along pretty soon. The juncos and white-crowned sparrows at the feeder are still here, but the males are in breeding plumage so I don't think they will be here much longer.

19th April 1990

Time to get the hummingbird feeders up! I had a male hummingbird at the flowers on my coral honeysuckle on Saturday afternoon and have had reports of several others. The females hang back for several weeks and we won't see many of them before the first week in May.

Ovenbirds, parula warblers, and yellow-throated warblers have arrived back from South America and are starting nests, but juncos and white-throated sparrows, our most common winter migrants, are still at my feeder. The whitethroats are giving their spring calls, so I expect to look out one morning soon and find them all gone.

We have been keeping a constant eye on the nesting wood duck. According to our reckoning, she should have been hatching out Easter morning. However, last Wednesday evening, while I was watching her through a telescope, a second female wood duck flew into the entrance, and there were two females on the nest. I watched: there appeared to be no conflict. In about five minutes the female who had been sitting on the eggs stood up, slipped out of the entrance, and flew away. The remaining female then settled on the eggs and arranged them to her satisfaction. I have not observed the two of them in the nest at the same time since, and as they look exactly alike I cannot be sure whether there are two females sharing incubation. If the two are sharing the nest, then all bets on the hatching date are off, since the second female's eggs were laid later.

3rd May 1990

Well, the wood duck eggs hatched on Easter Sunday, right on

WHITE-THROATED SPARROW
Zonotrichia albicollis

schedule, and we watched the little ducklings scurrying around the inside of the nest and over the mother's back. The mother kept them inside all of Easter day and brought them out on Monday morning. Unfortunately, we had to take our daughter to the airport and missed the jumping-out party. They were all out and gone when we returned in the early afternoon, so we don't know how many ducklings there were this year.

Sunday, April 22nd, as I was sitting in the yard, a female hummingbird began to gather spider silk from a dead weed about ten feet from my chair. As I watched, she collected a beakful and zoomed up to the top of a small beech tree at the edge of the driveway. There, on a small branch sixty-five feet up, she was constructing a nest. It looks complete now, and I expect she will begin incubating soon. This is a very early date for a hummingbird nest.

The bluebirds have competed their nest in a box at the edge of the garden and it has four eggs in it. Chickadees took over the box at the other edge of the garden and have hatched their brood. Friends from Nature Vision in Raleigh spent Sunday with us and, among other things, we videotaped the busy chickadee parents as they carried a continuous stream of green caterpillars into the nest to feed the hungry nestlings.

I think that I have found the approximate location of the nest of a very secretive cryptic little bird. Saturday, as I sat quietly at the edge of the driveway, a Louisiana waterthrush flew up and landed about four feet from me; I think it mistook me for a stump. It sat on a log, bobbing up and down like it was on a pogo stick for about twenty minutes, before flying into a clump of small shrubs and honeysuckle along the ditch bank. This bird builds a nest on the ground, usually in a hole among tree roots. If there is a nest there, it will be the first nest of this species I have seen. I am going to be very circumspect while I check it out. Incidentally, if you think watching birds isn't work, you try pretending to be a stump, not breathing or blinking for twenty minutes when a bird almost lands in your lap!

17th May 1990

An interesting little development is taking place in the beech tree in the side yard. After the wood duck and her brood left the day after Easter, the nest hollow remained empty for a week until a pileated woodpecker resumed roosting in it at night. Some time during the week, one of the numerous flying squirrels around the edge of the yard began to move leaves into the old nest. Then, a little over a week ago, another pair of wood ducks showed up in the yard and became very interested in the nest site. This is pretty late for wood ducks to nest, so this must be a pair whose first nesting was broken up and who want to re-nest.

This nest hole has two entrances, one about three feet above the other. When the female wood duck entered the lower, main, entrance and began to examine the old nest, turning and twisting, two flying squirrels popped out of the upper entrance. The female remained inside for about half an hour, then she and the male, who had been waiting patiently outside, flew off. The squirrels then returned inside. For the past week the wood ducks have been returning each morning, the female spending about an hour in the nest and chasing the flying squirrels out before leaving. From her actions, I think that she is laying a clutch of eggs. I would really like to know just what goes on in there. The wood duck is larger and more aggressive so she should be able to drive the flying squirrels out unless they have a side cranny they can move in to. For now we are watching to see how they work it out.

21st June 1990

The antics that go on each morning at the wood duck nest continue to amuse us. I think that the flying squirrels have given up and moved out, but the pileated woodpecker roosts each night on the side of the hollow just above the incubating hen wood duck and calls and drums around the nest entrance each morning before flying off to feed. A flicker arrives each morning and sits just outside the entrance hole calling loudly, furtively reaching in and pulling out leaves and down from the edge of the nest. The wood duck sits through it all. If she persists, we think that the eggs will hatch about June 22nd.

On Saturday evening a bluebird nestling either jumped or was pushed from the nest box. It had only pinfeathers and was way too young to be out of the nest. However, it was fed on the ground by the male and exposed to bright light for an hour or so. Whatever the reason, it refused to remain in the nest with the other two nestlings. I put it in several times, but the parents called and it tumbled out in response each time. I put the cat inside the house and put the nestling in a large planter with a tomato plant, and the male bluebird has been feeding it all day. After dark I'll get it and put it in a little box to keep inside during the night. Early in the morning I'll put it back in the planter so the male can feed it during the day. If it survives the regime, it should be fledged enough to make it after several days. Incidentally, while watching through the Celestron telescope as the male fed it, I saw that in addition to crickets he also gave it half a dozen small ground skinks. I had not previously realized that bluebirds would catch and eat small lizards.

27th August 1990

We continue to have hummingbirds at our feeders and will leave the feeders up probably into October. The instinct to migrate is very strong in migrating species such as the hummingbird, and the presence of feeders will not cause them to linger here until cold weather arrives.

After four years of outdoor exposure my main feeders are in a considerable state of disrepair and I will have to replace several of them during the next month. If you are thinking of putting up a winter feeder for the first time, there are several requirements needed to get birds to come to your feeder. First, birds will need an avenue of approach to the feeder that provides some cover. I solved this problem by making two simple tray feeders, nailing the trays on top of a wooden stake, and putting the stake in the ground at the edge of the nearest cover. When the birds found this feeder and had been using it for about a week, I put a second feeder up about twenty yards closer to the house, still keeping it near some cover; I put seeds in it and stopped putting seeds in the first feeder. The birds, used to coming to the first feeder, quickly found the second feeder and began using it. I then leap-frogged along a route that provided some cover, and was able to lead birds to my main feeder in about three weeks. Birds learn quickly and once they find your main feeder they will come directly to it. However, you will have to have some kind of cover near the feeder. Thick hedges or bushes are ideal. Lacking these, a brushpile four or five feet high and eight feet across, placed next the feeder, will work just as well. During the winter my brushpile is literally full of birds from dawn to dusk.

31st January 1991

I have to put in some time in the woodworking shop during the next month, courtesy of Byron Kehayes at the Edenton Housing Authority.

The wooden hollow pillars around the carports of the housing units are rotting at the base and are being replaced. They have been hauling them to the landfill, but it occurred to Mr Kehayes that they might be usable for bird or bat houses. He phoned me and I went to the Housing Authority office to look the discarded pillars over. I took twenty-four of them.

They are about eight feet tall with an interior diameter of about six inches, and will make excellent bird houses for a variety of small birds. I will cut them into nine-inch lengths, put a roof and bottom on them, and cut an entrance hole (one and a half inches for bluebirds, one and a quarter inches for white-breasted nuthatches and prothonotary warblers, and one inch for wrens, chickadees, and brown-headed nuthatches).

I'm also going to cut eighteen inches off the larger end of several pillars, plug both ends, cut a two-inch hole in one end, and mount it horizontally like a mailbox. I hope I can persuade a pair of great-crested flycatchers to move in. These are highly beneficial birds who need help in our area much more than bluebirds.

14th February 1991

I have what is developing into a problem with my bird feeders. I have at least three possums who show up at dusk to grub around under the feeders for spilled seed. This doesn't bother me as they are interesting to watch. However, they are also great nest robbers and can climb iron poles to bird boxes. I have a lot of nesting boxes around the house plus the wood duck who nests in the hollow beech in the side yard. I think that they're just going to have to go. I plan to try to live-trap them and then release them several miles away from my home.

28th March 1991

The wood duck is on her tenth day of incubation on her nest. I think that she is a different female from the last three years, because this one is more skittish.

Our big chocolate lab and I have worked out a system to rid us of some of the possums that have been raiding our bird feeders all winter. I open the door at 9 PM, he rushes around to all the feeders, catches a possum (if there is one), and brings it to me. I drop it in a burlap bag and take it for a three- or four-mile drive then release it, hoping it won't be able to find its way back.

30th May 1991

Now that our winter migrants have flown back north, it's pretty quiet around the seed feeder. With not so many numbers, we are getting to know the individual birds a little better.

We have two pairs of cardinals. One pair is very conventional. They fly in together, the female begs a bit at the edge of the feeder, the male husks sunflower seeds and feeds her, they feed quietly for a while, then leave together. The other pair's lifestyle is a bit more scandalous. To begin with, it's not a pair but a threesome, and although one of the males is dominant he has not been able to drive the extra male away. The female flies right in to the feeder and starts to feed while the males skirmish all around the yard and spend little time at the feeder. When the female leaves, they are both right behind her. I would like to find the nest to see if the extra male helps in raising the brood.

I have two pairs of titmice. One pair, regular as clockwork, comes to the feeder, each selects a sunflower seed and carries it to a sweet gum by the deck. Each bird has a favorite limb and a favorite spot on that limb. They go to the exact spot each time, face the same way, and proceed to husk and eat the seed. They will feed like this for twenty minutes or so, then it's back into the woods for an hour or so.

There is one pair of blue jays who arrive half a dozen times a day, create a lot of ruckus around the feeder, gobble a lot of seed, and zoom off through the woods. The female jay begs for food; sometimes the male feeds her, sometimes not.

The real bosses at the feeder are a pair of red-bellied woodpeckers. When they arrive they displace all the birds at the feeder. The female grabs a sunflower seed, hops along the feeder, and swings around to one end. She hangs there, pounds the seed into a crevice, and proceeds to open it. She will spend half an hour busily cracking seeds, not bothering anyone unless somebody gets in her way, in which case the offender is promptly driven off the feeder.

Friday morning a pair of prothonotary warblers showed up on the deck. They are one of only a few cavity-nesting warblers and their nesting habits are pretty much like Carolina wrens. The male is a bright yellow-orange with a little slate blue on his wings, the female a muted version of the male. They hopped all over the deck, peering into the house, investigating all the potted plants. I quickly put up two gourd nesting boxes, which the female found and investigated. They stayed around the rest of the day but did not show up Saturday or Sunday. They put in a brief appearance Monday, and I hear the male singing around the yard, so maybe there is a chance that they will nest here.

We have five female hummingbirds and one resident male around our hummingbird feeder, so there is a constant "hurrah" going on around it all day. The females are nesting close by. I've watched them gather cobwebs off the screens for nest-building and, while I know approximately where each nest is located, I haven't found one this year.

20th June 1991

Dave and Ginny Crowell just fledged two prothonotary warbler babies from their garage last Monday. The warbler parents moved in about a month ago, found a three-foot-tall stack of flower pots to their liking, and build a nest in the top pot. Dave left a back window open for the female, and in about thirteen days she hatched a clutch of eggs. Both parents fed the nestlings, not paying much attention to the Crowells, and when I went over last Monday both fledglings were out of the nest and learning to fly in the garage. The parents were trying to lure them outside with offerings of insects, but both babies were still in the garage when I left. They are going to be surprised to find out that the real world is a bit different from the garage they grew up in!

4th July 1991

The prothonotary warblers in Dave and Ginny's garage liked it so much that they are back, brooding a clutch of three eggs in a new nest they build in a short section of downspout standing on a bench near where the first nest was located. The eggs should hatch this week.

18th July 1991

From time to time hummingbirds get inside our greenhouse

and run out of energy before they can get out—I find them sitting almost comatose on the floor or bench. My solution is to pick up the hummingbird very gently and push the beak into a spoonful of the same sugar water that I put in the hummingbird feeder. The hummingbird will eventually start to suck up the sugar solution. I have had them sit on my opened hand and drink almost a spoonful of sugar water before flying away.

1st August 1991

I have a bluebird nesting box on a steel post at the edge of the garden, and a pair of bluebirds are raising a second brood in it. One evening last week as I sat in the back yard, the bluebird parents began to make a lot of racket in the garden, scolding and bill-popping and diving to the ground. I investigated and found a baby bluebird on the ground. It was much too young to be out of the nest, so I caught it and put it back in the nest box. The adults continued to scold, and in a minute or so the nestling jumped out of the nest box again. The adults flew down to it and began to bump it so that it hopped away from the vicinity of the nest box, continuing to give their former cries.

I went over and found a small (three-foot) black rat snake in the long grass at the base of the nest pole. I caught it just behind the head, carried it about three hundred yards down the driveway, and tossed it into the woods. As I carried it, it wrapped four coils around my hand and began to squeeze. Even though it was a small snake, the pressure on my hand was about the same as a very firm handshake.

I caught the nestling again and returned it to the nest box. It stayed this time, and the adults ceased to give their alarm calls and began to feed it. Apparently they had discovered the snake and were attempting to call the nestlings out of the box and cause them to scatter so the snake couldn't catch them all.

The next morning, as I sat on the deck, the same rat snake, minus the tip of his tail, came through the back yard and went into the woods on the other side of the house. That evening I heard the bluebirds scolding and bill-popping in the garden again, and upon investigating I found the nestling on the ground again with the parents calling and bumping it towards thick cover at the edge of the woods. I looked around, and sure enough there was the same rat snake in the grass near the nest box. I caught it again, and this time I took it for a car ride, releasing it about a mile away. I really don't know what the home range of a rat snake is, so I'm keeping a close watch to see if this one comes back again.

Meanwhile, I returned the baby bluebird to the nest box, where it stayed until it fledged last Saturday morning. I cleaned out the box when it left and found three unhatched bluebird eggs inside. For some reason, they were infertile, and only one nestling fledged from the second brood.

29th August 1991

I've been getting calls from people with hummingbird feeders, wondering when to take them down. I leave mine up until the end of November, and later if I see any late stragglers coming through.

The urge to migrate is the overriding drive in hummingbirds in the fall, and providing food for them will not cause them to linger until winter arrives. They put on about one third of their body weight in fat. With this as fuel they can fly all day, at an average speed of forty-two kilometers per hour, and cover five- to sixhundred kilometers non stop—enough to let them take overwater shortcuts across the Gulf of Mexico on their way south. By keeping your feeder in operation you may save the lives of hummingbirds who are migrating through very late in the season. I have a lot of hummingbirds around my feeders now, most of whom are migrators from farther north.

24th October 1991

It's been like a ghost town around my feeders for the last month.

The cardinals, titmice, chickadees, and nuthatches that have been around all summer have disappeared, temporarily I hope, but I don't remember this happening last year. I did see one chickadee this morning, but the sunflower seed in the feeders is mostly undisturbed.

28th November 1991

A few early white-throated sparrow migrants have shown up at the feeder this week, but as yet there isn't much activity. I'm busy reconstructing the brushpile by the feeder and raking leaves—lots of them!

16th January 1992

Our bird feeder is finally attracting its full complement of winter birds, with one glaring exception: we have had no cardinals at all this winter. Previous winters we have had four to five pairs at the feeders most of the day; as a matter of fact they were first at the feeder in early morning and the last to leave at dusk. Nuthatches are low too, and this disturbs me as both of these species are our local birds who nest here.

13th February 1992

The days are getting noticeably longer now, and a male bluebird has taken to perching on the bluebird box, fluttering his wings and giving his most seductive calls. The bluebirds at Harry and Marginette Lassiter's were observed carrying nesting material into their bluebird nesting box.

12th March 1992

The wood ducks have not shown up this spring at the hole in the beech tree where they have nested for the last four years. They are late, so perhaps something has happened to one or both of the pair. I checked out my bluebird boxes, and four of the seven are occupied by flying squirrels. A little tapping on the side brought the occupants to the entrance hole to stare at me with enormous soft eyes. Red-bellied and downy woodpeckers are excavating nest holes in dead trees around the yard, while a chickadee is excavating one in a stump in the garden.

A few wood warblers are passing through the woods, but all my winter birds are still around the feeders, as are lots of squirrels. Two late fall broods were raised in beech trees on either side of the house.

26th March 1992

Our winter birds are still here, the goldfinches mostly in their bright spring plumage and the juncos starting to sing their spring songs. Chickadees are using fiberglass insulation from my workshop to line their nests, a practice I'm not sure is wise.

4th June 1992

Last Sunday was too wet to play golf or work in the garden, so I carried a lawn chair down the driveway and sat down with binoculars to observe wildlife activity around the yard and garden. There is lots going on if one just takes the time to look.

A sudden commotion among the birds at the edge of the woods drew my attention, and I saw a black rat snake with half his body in one of my bird boxes, being scolded by flycatchers, bluebirds, chickadees, and wood thrushes. I went to the box and discovered not one but two rat snakes—one in the box, the other in a bush beside it, both about four feet long. I grabbed both of them and with a full arm swing tossed them about twenty yards back into the woods. I had thought this bird box was snake-proof, but during the last two years a branch had grown about two feet over it; the snake had climbed the tree, moved out on the limb, and extended itself down to the top of the box.

The box had a flying squirrel in it this spring, but when I removed the top to check inside I found the nest and four eggs of a great-crested flycatcher. The snake hadn't had time to swallow any eggs and had not been able to catch the female on the nest, so I put the top back on, trimmed away the overhanging branches, and in about three hours the female returned and entered the box to resume incubation.

Bluebirds are building a nest in the box in the garden, getting ready to raise a second brood. I found a new nest in low brush along the driveway. I think it belongs to a white-eyed vireo but will have to watch to find out for sure. A pair of blue-gray gnat-catchers were flitting up and down the driveway, and I'll watch to see if these tiny elegant birds decide to nest there.

16th July 1992

Black rat snakes are extraordinary climbers and nothing if not persistent. After I had pulled the two of them out of the nesting box, the flycatchers resumed incubation and hatched four young several days later. A week later I heard the adults scolding around the nest, and when I checked I found the same two snakes prowling around the nest box. I had pruned around the box on its pole so they could not climb a small tree and reach over to the nest box, and the box itself was on a metal pole that they could not climb.

I brought a folding chair out and watched their activities for an hour or so. They climbed small trees near the nest box and stretched out, trying to bridge the space from the tree to the box. Failing this, they both attempted to climb the metal pole, gave up, and then climbed vertically up the side of a big sweet gum nearby. They went up about thirty feet, slid out slowly on a small branch that reached over to brush against a limb of a maple tree, carefully shifted over to the maple branch, and climbed down the maple tree. On the way down, they eased out on every branch that projected over or towards the nest box, trying to reach it. Failing in this, they climbed to the ground and started the whole series over again. I stepped in at this point, caught them both, and released them about a mile away.

The flycatchers fledged the four young from the nest three days ago without any more trouble from this pair of snakes.

30th July 1992

I really enjoy the woods adjoining our ten acres and have been hoping that nothing would change. Two weeks ago I was awakened by the sound of heavy equipment, and when I went back I found that the thirty acres to the south of us were being logged. In the last two weeks the entire thirty acres have been clearcut. Everything four inches and over in diameter was cut and everything smaller has been crushed and ground up by the skidders and other heavy equipment. The big hollow beech trees have all been cut and at last sighting were still lying where they fell. I don't know if they will be utilized or just cut up and bulldozed into windrows. I don't know for sure, but the area will probably be replanted to pine.

Pure pine stands are not natural in the coastal plains and are an abomination to biologists. All the plants, animals, birds, and other biota that evolved with the hardwood forests over millions of years cannot survive in pure pine plantations. There is a lot of food for wildlife in young pine plantations, but as soon as the canopy closes in—about six years—the food supply dries up, bird and animals leave, and nothing competes with the pines except sweet gums.

Populations of the wildflowers that grew in the logged block also grow in our woods, and the displaced wildlife will now move into our woods and the woods to the east. However, birds and animals need room for core territories, and about half of the wildlife that was formerly here will lose out. This is particularly critical for woodland birds. Their populations are already down, and there is a lot of concern about their chances of survival in our increasingly fragmented hardwood forests.

As a naturalist I am dismayed by the continuing impoverishment of our environment and by the blindness of people who cannot see that impoverishment of our environment will lead to impoverishment of our lives. Perhaps we should think about bulldozing out some of the pine plantations and replanting some of our native hardwood forests.

22nd October 1992

Tree swallows are moving through, and I see several species of wood warblers in transit through our woods, but the main group of our winter migrants has not started arriving yet.

5th November 1992

More of our winter birds are showing up. This week I captured a winter wren in our greenhouse. This tiny bird is much smaller and darker than our Carolina wren, and its short tail is cocked forward to almost touch the back of its head. It is almost more mouse than bird, spending its time foraging around logs and brushpiles. They are rarely seen, and this was only the second or third time I have had one in my hands.

19th November 1992

Cardinals, white-throated sparrows, juncos, titmice, chickadees, nuthatches, towhees, and purple finches are regular visitors to our feeders now. Several brown creepers are active in the woods, and hermit thrushes have taken up winter residence in the woods as well. A phoebe has been around the yard all morning, and last Thursday a very late redstart, one of our more striking warblers, was foraging along the edge of the garden.

21st January 1993

We seem to have more birds at our feeder this winter, but just the usual species so far: juncos, white-throated and chipping sparrows, chickadees, nuthatches, cardinals, woodpeckers, goldfinches, and purple finches. Several pairs of bluebirds have been investigating our nest boxes these last two mornings but are not too serious yet.

4th February 1993

Our bird feeders continue to be crowded. We have so many goldfinches that I have to refill the sunflower seed feeder every morning. Back in the woods here, we never get any house finches, but friends in town are having a lot of them show up at their feeders. This bird, a western species introduced into the east in

1940, is rapidly expanding its range east of the Mississippi and may out-compete the English sparrow and reduce its numbers.

Chickadees have excavated roosting cavities in two tall stumps in the yard, and I'm curious to see if they will nest in them this spring.

18th February 1993

Last week I had a flush of cardinals at my feeders. I counted eight males and four females. They hung around for several days and then moved on. I wonder if other feeders in the area showed a similar increase.

4th March 1993

I spent several hours last Sunday trying to photograph a group of palm warblers in the field along our driveway. They are tiny birds who creep around in the grass pumping their tails vigorously, consistently refusing to let me get close enough to get a good photograph. They will hang around for several more weeks yet, so I haven't given up on them.

15th April 1993

It's time to put out the hummingbird feeders. Bob and Mabel Frost had a hummingbird in their yard last week and we had one at our red camellia on Monday just at dusk. Camellias are not their favorite flower, but that's about all that's available right now. I put up our feeder and the little male hummer flew up and tanked up just before dark.

Bluebirds are definitely nesting in one of our nest boxes, and chickadees are using the one the bluebirds used last year. Most of our juncos and white-throated sparrows have left for their northern breeding ground, so activity at our feeders has tapered off slightly. We still have large numbers of chipping sparrows and goldfinches, some of the latter in full spring plumage. Ovenbirds are singing in our woods and they will be nesting in a month or so.

On the debit side, cowbirds have also arrived. Our deciduous woodland birds are already under considerable stress from habitat destruction, and the increasing influx of cowbirds may be the straw that breaks the camel's back. A lot of biologists are looking into the cowbird problem, and I hope we get some management recommendations from them soon.

29th April 1993

In the deciduous woods around our house we have several pairs of ovenbirds singing, and for the past several days two or three red-eyed vireos have joined the chorus. The ovenbirds build a nest in the leaves on the ground, and the red-eyed vireos build a neat, tightly woven nest high up in the tops of trees.

We have a pair of great-crested flycatchers calling around the yard and in the woods; they are hole nesters and I have put up several boxes for them, but they are fussy nesters and about half the time will use an abandoned woodpecker nest back in the woods. When they do nest in the yard they are interesting to watch. Last year, in feeding their young the female brought only moths and dragonflies and the male brought only large grasshoppers.

The female bluebird is incubating eggs in a nest box in the front yard; they should hatch in a day or so. We are going to have to keep a sharp eye on the nest. The parents picked a box that is accessible to rat snakes, and one about four feet long was observed sunning itself on the roof of my workshop close to the nest-box location.

3rd June 1993

I received calls this week from friends having trouble with rat snake predation among their bird houses. In both cases it was chickadee nests which were raided and the young taken. Rat snakes are persistent and skillful climbers, and there are three ways to foil them: mount the nesting box on the side of the house or shed away from wires and vines; mount the nesting box on a telephone pole and keep the vines away; or mount the nesting box on steel or plastic pipe. All of my nest boxes are mounted on steel pipes, and I have enjoyed watching persistent rat snakes spend hours trying to climb them.

17th June 1993

As we were leaving the parking area of our driveway last week a dead limb fell from an overhanging tree and landed in front of the car. We stopped, and Dorothy got out to remove the limb. As she moved it we noticed a hummingbird nest plastered to it. It was a new nest, so we began to search for eggs or young birds. We soon found a young hummingbird crouched in the gravel and, after more searching, a second one who had been killed by the fall. I took the branch with the nest on it and nailed it to the tree as high as I could reach, then replaced the live nestling. It began to call faintly, and in an hour or so the female came to it and began to feed it. We watched it for the next four days until it fledged Saturday morning. Its mother will continue to feed it for several days until it learns to feed on its own. I expect to see it at our feeder with its mother soon.

16th September 1993

We are just back from vacation. I refilled all of our feeders and by evening all the birds were back, the chickadees and titmice scolding us for neglecting them, and the hummingbirds busy squabbling among themselves. A few warblers have shown up passing through the woods: a black-and-white hung around for a day or so, and a pair of redstarts spent a morning around our bird bath before moving on.

30th September 1993

Hummingbird numbers at my feeders are beginning to drop, but we're still getting two or three a day. These don't hang around and squabble like the summer residents, but tank up a few times then head on south.

I'm seeing a few warblers coming through the woods: red-starts, orange-crowned, and ovenbirds. An ovenbird got trapped in the greenhouse, and while trying to capture and release it I saw that it was banded. Unfortunately it escaped before I could capture it and read its band number. I have banded these birds in New York State and was very curious about where this one had been banded.

We have about seven cardinals active at our feeder, four of them juveniles, and two goldfinches showed up on Sunday morning. I'll have to get my thistle feeder up to try to hold them here as well as any pine siskins who might show up with them. The pair of resident barred owls in our woods are becoming quite vocal at night, and one has shown up in the back yard in the afternoon.

4th November 1993

I haven't seen a hummingbird for several weeks, so I put my hummingbird feeders away at the end of October. Our seed feeders are still very active with chickadees, titmice, nuthatches, and cardinals. One very bright-plumaged goldfinch has been showing up for the last week, but none of the juncos and sparrows nor any of the other winter migrants have shown up yet.

I know that winter is coming, as the big pileated woodpeckers in our woods have returned to their winter roost in the big hollow beech in the side yard, and grey squirrels are cutting twigs and building a winter nest in a hollow in the big beech in the garden. Looks like I'll have to cease being a grasshopper and become an ant and start cutting our winter firewood!

18th November 1993

I've heard a screech-owl around the yard for the last two nights. I had to suspend putting out peanut butter for flying squirrels because I was attracting several owls who perched in trees near the feeders and attempted to prey on the flying squirrels. This miniature version of the horned owl will take flying squirrels but is primarily a mouser, with an appetite for large flying moths too. I have found the wings of over a dozen luna moths in our driveway over the years.

2nd December 1993

From the looks of things, the wintering birds at our feeders are going to need all the cover they can get: a sharp-shinned hawk has taken to hanging around the yard in hopes of catching small birds as they visit the feeders. It's pretty wary, however, and the presence of anyone outside will scare it away.

Carolina wrens are very adaptable little birds, even foolhardy at times. One has begun to forage for spiders in our greenhouse, and to keep from trapping it inside I keep one of the sliding doors open about four inches. I have several hanging baskets of flowers in the greenhouse and the wren has decided that one of them is just the place to roost for the night. Our cat also spends the night in the greenhouse, and although the wren is safe up in the flowerpot, it is at risk when it decides to forage very early in the morning.

13th January 1994

We have lots of cardinals, goldfinches, purple finches, juncos, chickadees, titmice, nuthatches, white-throated sparrows, and red-bellied woodpeckers. Half a dozen Carolina wrens hang around the feeders—just throwing out seeds, as far as I can tell. The last two days we have had two female evening grosbeaks at our sunflower feeders, so maybe this will be a winter-finch winter when bad weather and a scarcity of food force these birds to winter much farther south than usual.

17th February 1994

The cold weather has pushed lots of birds to our feeders. I counted over sixty-five goldfinches in a feeding frenzy last Saturday. Some of the males are beginning to change to their spring plumage and are sporting splashes of brilliant yellow.

The evening grosbeaks still show up at least once a day: three bright-yellow, white, and black males and four more subdued plumaged females. They rule the roost whenever they are in the feeder, and all the other birds give them a wide berth. Having been bitten by them during mist-netting* activities in the past, I can see why. Our favorite ploy when removing grosbeaks from the net was to give them a pencil to bite; they can dent a wooden pencil almost enough to break it. Only the remembrance of our own anguish when bitten prevented us from breaking up at the antics and profanity of a colleague trying to persuade a struggling grosbeak to let go!

Some birds are in short supply this winter. I rarely see towhees, and have only one fox sparrow and an occasional blue jay. We have fewer white-throated sparrows and juncos, about the same number of chickadees, and slightly more titmice.

17th March 1994

Bluebirds, chickadees, and titmice are beginning to build nests in our boxes. I've put up some new ones, as well as one specifically designed for great-crested flycatchers.

Our feeders are overflowing with goldfinches this spring, a few males in full breeding plumage, and the half dozen or so evening grosbeaks still stop by now and then. The goldfinches and grosbeaks won't be around much longer. I hope our last seventy-five pounds of bird seed will last as long as they stay.

5th May 1994

All of my nesting woodland birds are back, with the exception of wood thrushes and Acadian flycatchers. The male great-crested

---

* Mist nets are very fine-meshed black nylon nets about thirty feet by six feet. They have a stiffening cord top and bottom plus three in between. A lane about four feet wide is cut through a hedgerow or in the woods where birds move. The net is stretched between two poles down the center of the lane. Birds can't see the net and fly into it, punching little pockets in the fine mesh and getting entangled. They are carefully untangled, put into a holding cage, and taken to a central location where they are weighed, sexed, species determination made, and any other data taken. They are then banded with a tiny numbered Fish and Wildlife aluminum band and released. Recovery of bands over the years gives biologists information about the distribution and migration pattern of each species. Bird banders are licensed by the Federal Government and the licenses are not easy to acquire.

flycatcher has been here for weeks and was joined Saturday by a female. The two have been checking out a nesting box that I put up for them at the edge of the woods. I have two nesting pairs of bluebirds and one pair of chickadees in boxes in the yard, and a lone male prothonotary warbler has been hanging around the house for three weeks vainly trying to attract a female and has even started several nest sites in a couple of nesting boxes.

A pair of summer tanagers arrived together last week and the male has been singing constantly around the yard. A wood-pewee is calling around the yard; this is a mixed blessing as last year she destroyed a hummingbird nest and a summer tanager nest, using the materials to build her own. A pair of blue-gray gnatcatchers are spending a lot of time each morning in the garden and I've been sitting out with binoculars trying to find the nest. It's very tiny and looks much like a hummingbird nest; I would love to find one to photograph.

Last week I discovered that a pair of neck-banded Canada geese have nested in the forty acres of big deciduous woods that were logged behind our house a couple of years ago. The female is incubating a clutch of eggs on a nest on a stump pile in the middle of a totally devastated area piled high with downed trees and branches.

26th May 1994

For the past week I've had a pair of blue-gray gnatcatchers foraging around in the garden. I suspected that they had a nest close by, so Friday morning I sat quietly with binoculars in the side yard and watched them for two hours, finally locating their nest: about ninety feet up in a small fork in the top of a sweet gum tree. I saw them carrying up nesting material, and with the aid of my 45x telescope I could watch them tuck in small bits of plant fibers. The nest itself is almost as small as a hummingbird's nest—about the size of a walnut—and like a hummingbird's nest it is covered with lichens. Unfortunately it is much too high to photograph.

With the arrival of the wood thrushes last week the roster of our summer woodland birds is complete, and the medley of their morning songs is a delight.

9th June 1994

I'm still enjoying watching nesting birds around the yard. The blue-gray gnatcatchers are incubating eggs in their high nest in the top of the tall sweet gum and the red-eyed vireos are doing the same a little lower down. An indigo bunting pair that have been hanging around the garden have started a nest in the short weeds and brush at the edge of the garden, and I've managed to get several close-ups of the male while he's acting territorial.

We have three female hummingbirds coming to our feeder, and by bee-lining them as they leave the feeder I know roughly where their nests are but have yet to actually locate one precisely. Wood thrushes, crested flycatchers, wood-pewees, Acadian flycatchers, summer tanagers, and ovenbirds are singing and calling around the yard and garden but are nesting a little farther back in the woods. Bluebirds, chickadees, titmice, and nuthatches use the nesting boxes we put up, and red-bellied and pileated woodpeckers nest back in the woods, but we are too far back in the woods to get any of what I call yard birds: the mockingbirds, thrashers, cardinals, catbirds, house finches, orioles, and robins.

15th September 1994

We still have a few hummingbirds coming to our feeder. They are not as belligerent as the summer ones, so I think these are migrants putting on weight and stocking up on energy as they head for the Gulf of Mexico and their long flight to their winter range in Mexico and South America.

13th October 1994

We have both great horned and barred owls in our woods, and they are very vocal at this time of year. At least once a day, one or other of them is discovered by crows who seemingly become hysterical. The resulting uproar draws in crows from miles around. Listening to the racket, I can tell just what the owl is doing. If he pretends the crows are not there, it's not much fun for them and they lose interest, become quiet, and soon leave, letting the owl settle his feathers and doze off again. However, if the owl moves or flies, every crow sounds off and the racket abruptly rises in volume. The crows are careful to stay well out of his reach, but possibly the owl might get revenge by raiding a crow roost at night and making off with one.

Warblers are migrating through our area and have been for the last month or so. Unfortunately, a small percentage of them fly into picture windows and break their necks. I collect as many of these as I can and send them to the museum in Raleigh, where they are added to the study collection. Most I can identify, but fall warblers are confusing and difficult to pin down as to species. I have two in the freezer now. One is an ovenbird, found on our side deck. The other is a very puzzling one which hit the window at our daughter Toby's house on Country Club Drive. It does not match any warbler in the books that I have. The closest match is to a fall-plumaged Bachman's warbler. The area is right but it is the rarest bird in North America. It will probably turn out to be an unusual fall morph of one of our common warblers.

27th October 1994

I'm putting away my hummingbird feeder, not having seen a hummingbird for several weeks. Our seed feeders have been very inactive for several weeks now, just a few cardinals and chickadees, but Sunday morning a lone junco showed up. This week I'll get a bag of white millet and make my standard mixture for winter birds: half black sunflower seed to half white millet. This mix seems to be the best for us.

There seems to be a disease among house finches that is killing a lot of them in the western United States. It shows up as huge ulcers on their heads. A few cases have been reported here, and

AMERICAN CROW
Corvus brachyrhynchos

I'm trying to find out more about it. If it shows up here and proves to be highly contagious, we might all better disinfect our feeders and cease feeding activities until the seriousness of the problem can be ascertained.

17th November 1994

A flock of wild turkeys have taken up residence in our woods. There are fifteen in the flock and every evening, regular as clockwork, they cross our driveway on the way to their roost. In the morning about 7 AM they amble through our yard eating acorns and beechnuts. If we stay well away from the windows they will linger for fifteen or twenty minutes before passing through to the woods, but if they see anyone move they're off in a flash. They are big, beautiful birds, apparently just recently introduced into Chowan County in the hopes that they will multiply and be available to hunt sometime in the future. But for now they are just "purty" to watch and enjoy.

8th December 1994

We haven't seen the flock of wild turkeys for a week or so. Last week a bobcat caught and killed one in our driveway and the rest took off and haven't been back.

The woods are pretty quiet. Not too many winter birds at the feeders yet.

5th January 1995

The wild turkey flock showed up again last week in the woods along our side yard. There were eight birds in the flock, and this is the first I've seen of them since the bobcat caught one in the driveway. They were foraging for beechnuts and acorns among the fallen leaves but were very alert, so the bobcat may still be around.

Our bird feeders are reasonably active now: lots of white-throated sparrows and juncos, but low on cardinals, chipping sparrows, titmice, chickadees, and nuthatches. So far I have had no goldfinches, siskins, or towhees. We do have four fox sparrows. This largest of our sparrows, beautifully marked with big reddish-brown splotches, does not show up at our feeder every year, and I have been trying to get close-up photographs of them for the past several days.

26th January 1995

A pair of pileated woodpeckers have become interested in the two big hollow beech trees in our side yard and are coming to roost in them regularly each evening. Oddly enough, they are accompanied by a pair of flickers, and the two pairs bicker and squabble over the roost sites, the pileateds always having first pick. The tree favored by the pileated is one that European hornets used last year, and the big woodpecker seems to enjoy tearing out the hornet nest and tossing it out of the hole. A Carolina wren has also elected to roost in the old hornet's nest and comes out fussing and bustling about until the pileated ceases work and settles down for the night, when it will sneak back in and settle down too.

I had removed several second- and third-story window screens so I could photograph these activities and was doing so Saturday evening, when I looked down and discovered the flock of wild turkeys scratching in the leaves at the base of the tree. They were not aware of me, and I quickly exposed half a roll of film as they worked through the woods. They are beautiful birds, sleek and shiny, twelve in the flock, two down from the fourteen we had seen earlier in the year. They passed through at the same time Sunday evening. They are creatures of habit, so I hope they get set in this routine. I'd like the opportunity to photograph and observe them and perhaps get a crew down to videotape them.

They moved on around the house and I went to a window on the north side to keep track of them, and was watching when a large meteor passed across the whole northern horizon pretty high up. It had a long bright trail and broke into several pieces before it winked out in the western sky. I heard no sound, so it was probably a hundred miles or so high and at least that far away. It happened at around 5:30 PM. It could have been a satellite falling out of orbit, or a meteor; in any case it was the brightest object I have ever seen burning up in the atmosphere.

16th February 1995

We have five species of woodpecker drumming in our woods almost every morning, and I hope they will all nest here this summer. Probably only one pair of each species, however, as our woods are only ten acres, and like most birds they are intolerant of crowding from their own species during nesting season.

2nd March 1995

We have been getting a lot of enjoyment out of watching the wild turkeys during the last month. In the last two weeks they have shifted their roost to the big trees around the edge of our yard. They fly down to the ground about half past six in the morning, come running in single file to several big beech trees at the edge of the yard, and scratch around in the leaves for an hour or so before moving through the yard and into the woods west of the house. We won't see them again until about five o'clock, when they come running through the woods up to the yard and begin foraging among the beech leaves.

They like the fresh grass and chickweed in the yard and flower beds, and come right to the edge of the deck to peck the greenery and scratch among the leaves. They like buds, and have eaten all the flower buds from our rhododendrons. Last week a red fox dashed in among them and attempted to catch one. They saw the fox in plenty of time and all flew up in the trees.

They are extremely wary. We have to keep the lights turned off in the house and move slowly, taking care not to skyline ourselves against a window on the other side of the room and not to make any noise. One time while they were in the yard Dorothy knocked over a bottle of olive oil in the kitchen, and the turkeys ran into the woods at high speed. They are very curious, however, and were soon back. They are fascinated by the television, coming up to the edge of the deck and peering into the window. We keep the volume low and, while extremely alert, they appear more puzzled than frightened.

At about 6 PM they begin to work their way into the woods at the edge of the yard, forage there a bit, then one by one take a short run, take off, and fly up into the tops of tall trees to roost for the night. They are seventy to eighty feet up, one or two to a tree, a few in pines but mostly hardwoods. They move around finding comfortable perches, but soon settle down for the night. I haven't the faintest idea what they think of our lighted house, or why they shifted their roost so close to the house in the first place.

This does give me an unparalleled opportunity to observe a free-ranging flock at very close range. There are four young gobblers in the flock; two are more brightly colored, are dominant, and tend to strut and display in the morning. The flock appears to have periods of play when they suddenly dart about like minnows, leap into the air, and flap their wings, then, as suddenly, go back to feeding. Several of the hens will scratch around our bird feeder and will chase away squirrels who come close. On Sunday evening they were all in the yard when a red-tailed hawk flew close over them and landed in the tree overhead. The turkeys erected their breast-, back-, and neck-feathers—effectively doubling their size—and watched the hawk closely. When it lost interest and flew off, they immediately slimmed down again and resumed foraging.

The turkeys are really curtailing our social life. We can't leave the house before 8 AM and have to be home by 4:30 PM. We ask visitors to follow the same schedule!

23rd March 1995

Frenetic activity in the garden and yard these past few sunny mornings.

We have eight bird nesting boxes up around the house. Built to bluebird specifications, with a hole one and an half inches in diameter, they are also acceptable to chickadees, titmice, and nuthatches—not to mention flying squirrels: one has squatter's rights to a nest box at the edge of the woods. All the hole-nesting birds mentioned above are interested in the boxes, but only the chickadees are serious at this time. The bluebirds are the most aggressive, chasing the others away in a bill-popping fury from the boxes they used last year. The persistent little chickadees have claimed one and are building a nest in it.

There was a lot of commotion around the box occupied by the flying squirrel Saturday evening. Five brilliant bluebird males were perched close to the entrance, taking turns hovering just in front of the entrance hole and roundly cursing the flying squirrel who had his head out resolutely blocking the entrance. It was roosting time, and the bluebirds were looking for a place to roost. I have found as many as six male bluebirds crammed into one nest box on cold nights.

Five species of woodpecker are actively drumming in the woods, but I don't think that any are actually drilling a nest hole. A pair of pileated woodpeckers are enlarging cavities in two big beech trees in the side yard, but I think that they are only using them for roosting. They are actively foraging around the yard, however, giving me excellent opportunities to photograph them.

The turkeys are still active around the yard mornings and evenings and go to roost in the trees near the house almost every night. One actually walked up the steps and onto the deck the other night! Watching them carefully through the binoculars I have been able to spot a band on one of the hens. All the turkeys released by the Game Department were banded before release. None of the rest of the flock is banded, so I think that the banded hen is the mother of the entire flock. If so, she must be an exceptional mother to successfully raise such a large brood. Of course, the flock may be composed of the broods of two hens and something may have happened to one of them, or I may not have been able to spot the other banded hen yet.

13th April 1995

Mike Dunn came over last week with his television camera and we took a lot of footage of the turkeys foraging and the gobblers strutting. The two gobblers are amusing: one is clearly dominant, gets to do all the mating, and has a much fancier strut.; they stay close together all the time and are the only ones now who roost in trees. The hens now number five and are nesting separately; they forage quickly and soon slip back to their nests, where they spend the night.

Bluebirds and chickadees are nesting in boxes in the garden, and a pair of Carolina wrens have made a nest in a desk on the deck. This year a pair of wood ducks are nesting again in the hollow beech tree in the side yard. I've seen the female several times. She is very shy and almost literally goes in the nest hole on the fly.

27th April 1995

I've been getting a lot of calls about birds these last few weeks. Many are concerned about birds and windows, and the answer is simple. Male birds, particularly bluebirds, cardinals, and prothonotary warblers, see their reflection in windows, think it is a rival male in their territory, and attempt to drive him out; in the process they can make a mess of entire windows. They will come back several times a day to chase the perceived male away. The remedy is to put a piece of paper over the pane or stretch a ribbon across the window—anything to block the mirror effect or break up the image.

I've also had a lot of calls about baby birds. They fall or are pushed out of nests and pose a dilemma for tender-hearted persons who find them. If it has feathers, let it alone: the parent birds know where it is and will continue to feed it. If it is naked and helpless you have three options: by far the best is to put it back into the nest, if possible; if not, you can harden your heart and let nature take its course; or you can try to rear it yourself. Rearing young birds is a very daunting task. Most require several soft-bodied insects every ten minutes or so throughout the day and will not survive on any substitute. I have reared young hawks and owls but gave up on songbirds long ago.

11th May 1995

In the early mornings our deciduous woods are full of birdsong: ovenbirds, wood thrushes, great-crested flycatchers, red-eyed and white-eyed vireos, wood-pewees, Acadian flycatchers, summer tanagers, and several unseen warbler species high in the trees. Bluebirds, titmice, wrens, chickadees, and hummingbirds are nesting in and around the yard. Spring is our favorite time to be in deciduous woods.

The two wild turkey gobblers still show up in the yard several times a week and we are hoping that one of the hens will hatch and bring her brood along so I can get some photographs.

The Dickensons of Arrowhead Beach dropped off an interesting bird's nest last week. It had fallen out of a tree in their yard. The nest was that of a wood thrush and the entire base was constructed of Saran wrap. These birds often build into their nests the shed skins of snakes, and strips of plastic and paper are acceptable substitutes.

25th May 1995

Bluebirds are doing very well this spring. The pair in our garden fledged four from their nest just last week, the Saunders at their new home on Route 32 South report that the pair nesting in their back yard are feeding a brood, and four more young just fledged from a nest box at Toby's home on Country Club Drive. Another nest box in her yard has been taken over by a pair of great-crested flycatchers. We peered in the box last week and could see the tiny red gaping maws of the newly hatched young as they begged for food.

The wild turkeys still show up in the yard almost every day and are still very wary. If one of us steps outside the house, they run off like greyhounds and disappear for the rest of the day.

21st September 1995

We have been getting increasing numbers of migrant humming-birds at our feeder during the past two weeks. By the time they reach Florida and the Gulf Coast, they will have put on about a third more body weight for their over-water flight to Cuba, the Bahamas, and Mexico. They don't, as old wives' tales say, cling to the feathers of other birds and hitch a ride across the Gulf of Mexico! Neither do they fly directly across the Gulf. At their average speed of twenty-seven miles per hour the shortest cross-ing, 550 miles, would take about eighteen hours. None of our data on the Rubythroat suggests that it ever flies after dark. It is more probable that most of them skirt the Gulf with short hops over water along the Louisiana and Texas coasts, and that a good number of east-coast hummers cross to Cuba from Florida and then on to Mexico and South America in short island hops, none longer than about five hours.

I have colored tapes and red handles on some of my tools in the greenhouse workshop, and I'm continually having to gently shoo out hummingbirds who come in to investigate the bright colors. Last week, while weeding the garden, a buzzing distur-bance in the long grass proved to be a hummingbird and a bald-face hornet grappling and rolling over and over in the grass. When I disturbed them they separated and flew off in opposite directions. I don't know what the fracas was all about , but I suspect that the hornet mistook the hummingbird for a large moth and was attempting to kill it and feed it to young hornets. Certainly a hornet sting could kill a hummingbird.

Lots of wood warblers are passing through just now, all busily stocking up fat reserves for their over-water flights to South America, and unusually quiet. They are in their fall plumage now, quite nondescript, and hard to identify. You have to sit quietly and keep a sharp eye out to see them at all. One of them, an ovenbird, got into the greenhouse last week. I found it sedately walking across the floor and was able to capture and release it unharmed into the woods.

5th October 1995

The little kestrel who winters along our driveway is back. He sat on the electric wire this morning pulling apart a field mouse he had just caught.

9th November 1995

Our feeders are becoming a bit more active now. A few early juncos are regular visitors, and this morning I saw a white-throated sparrow in the feeder just outside the kitchen window. The resident chickadees, titmice, nuthatches, and cardinals are also becoming more active around the feeders. The wild turkeys continue to forage through our yard almost every day. Our puppy, Tanner, watches them intently through the sliding glass doors as long as they are in sight.

In the woods the birds are scattered out and I have to actively hunt them out. In the past week I have seen black-throated blue warblers, redstarts, pine warblers, black-and-white warblers, and several small nondescript warblers that I could not see well enough to identify.

14th December 1995

The vanguard of our wintering robins came through our woods last week. They foraged through the leaves on the lawn most of the day but were more interested in the ripe dogwood berries and just about stripped our trees. Seeing a major part of their winter food supply vanishing, the bluebirds and flickers joined in the feast, and later in the morning a pileated woodpecker hung upside down at the end of a branch, stuffing himself.

This has the makings of a good winter-finch year, a year when for some reason—bad weather or failure of the conifer seed crop—a lot of winter finches erupt far south of their usual winter range. A week ago I heard an evening grosbeak calling in our woods. A day later Dorothy saw three of them at our feeder, and last Sunday as I was working in the greenhouse thirty-two of them descended on our two feeders. They stayed about an hour, cleaning out both feeders. They are big beautiful aggressive birds. Of our local species only the red-bellied woodpecker would stand his ground in a confrontation with them. I banded them when we lived in New York State and had to wear heavy gloves to protect my fingers from their huge powerful beaks.

A few marsh hawks are coursing over our fields now, and the little kestrel who spends the winter hunting mice along our driveway is back and in business. About half the time we see him he has a mouse clutched in one foot and is eating it like an ice-cream cone.

11th January 1996

The large flock of evening grosbeaks continue to visit our feeders. They are hooked on sunflower seed: I am going through my third twenty-five-pound bag. Right now they are giving us cause for concern. They are fast erratic flyers, given to sudden alarms when small flocks leave the feeder at high speed and whirl away over the woods. As they lift over the house, several small flocks and individuals have attempted to fly through the reflection in a second-story window. Five have broken their necks, and repose in our freezer awaiting a trip to the museum; we have successfully treated half a dozen more and released them to rejoin their flock. We have paper cut-outs glued to the window to deter this sort of accident, but I'm going to have to put large paper streamers on the outside of the windows and hope that this will deter them from attempting shortcuts through the house.

I have reports of over-wintering hummingbirds from Kill

Devil Hills, from Hatteras, and from the feeders at the Babeaux home on Montpelier Drive. There is renewed interest in these over-wintering hummingbirds and a lot of debate about the species involved.

One would expect these stragglers to be our breeding species, the ruby-throated hummingbird, but from captured or dead specimens the consensus is that hummingbirds seen in the south east in winter are more likely to be black-chinned humming-birds; females and immatures of these two species, however, cannot be separated in the field. A more likely possibility is the rufous hummingbird. Both the black-chinned and the rufous leave Mexico in the spring, go on into Canada to breed, then some of them, instead of returning south to Mexico, head east across Canada to Nova Scotia, south down the east coast to Florida, then across to Texas and Mexico. It is these birds that we see here in the winter.

Incidentally, hummers need protein to remain healthy, so to the sugarwater of these winter hummers dissolve a ten-grain capsule of gelatin and add it to the mixture.

25th January 1996

The large flocks of evening grosbeaks continue to visit our feeders, and in spite of all the paper twisters in front of the windows they continue to fly into them. I now have eleven birds in my freezer: nine females, two males.

8th February 1996

During this frigid weather the activity around our feeders has increased tenfold. I fill the feeders three times a day and almost have to brush the birds away to do so. Most of the birds now are Redwings, grackles, and goldfinches. The grosbeaks are still numerous, and I even have a few pine siskins. Now is a particularly interesting time to sit back and observe feeder activity.

14th March 1996

The weather in these waning days of winter is notoriously fickle, with temperature swings of thirty degrees from one day to the next—balmy breezes from the south one day, and so cold the next that you think that all that stands between you and the North Pole is a barbed-wire fence. We humans mind this and complain bitterly when forced back inside by a sudden cold front. Outside, however, nature's heart never misses a beat.

Bird migrations are governed by day length not temperature, and our winter visitors are beginning to leave us for their summer breeding grounds. The kestrels and marsh hawks have almost all left, and daily big flocks of tundra swans fly over the house, trumpeting loudly as they line up their vee formations and head north.

We still get small flocks of evening grosbeaks at the feeder but nothing like the huge numbers that would empty the feeder every day during January and February. The fox sparrows, who nest in Labrador, have mostly left; juncos and white-throated sparrows are still here but the whitethroat males are sporting spring court-ing plumage and are tentatively beginning to whistle softly their *Poor Sam Peabody-Peabody* call, so they will be leaving before long. Goldfinches are looking a little more yellow at the feeder now as the males begin to moult towards their summer plum-age. The males of our most numerous wintering warblers, the yellow-rumped, are just beginning to get their spring plumage; we won't see them in their full glory here.

Some of our birds who migrated to the tropics for the winter are showing up. Last Saturday I saw a male purple martin sitting on telephone wires out at Somerset Farm, and Fred Inglis saw an osprey along the Sound the day before. Early male humming-birds will start showing up in late March—it's time to get feeders ready!

28th March 1996

The wild turkeys are back with us in a big way this spring. There are twelve of them, six hens and six gobblers; two of the gobblers are mature birds with long beards, the other four are Jakes with little short beards. Both of the big gobblers are strutting and gobbling in the woods now.

Saturday afternoon at about 4 PM I was out on our deck working away on a piece of sculpture with adz and chisels, making a lot of chips and noise in the process. I looked up, and coming through the edge of the woods about twenty-five yards away were all twelve of the turkeys. I stopped working and watched as they came up around our bird feeders and began scratching in the leaves. This has happened to me twice in the last two weeks. If I'm sitting or working in one place in the yard or on the deck, and even if I'm making a lot of racket, the turkeys apparently are not really alarmed—they are aware of me and have been long before I see them. If I come out of the house after they are here, however, it's a different story—they hightail it back into the woods as soon as I'm out the door.

Last Saturday when they appeared I ceased my activity and very slowly sat down on the deck and leaned back against a bench. The hens and four young gobblers began to scratch among the leaves but the two big gobblers headed across the yard towards the greenhouse, one end of which was about fifteen feet from where I sat. They began pecking the glass doors to the greenhouse, walking from one end to the other. I thought at first that they were catching flies, but what they were actually doing was fighting their reflections in the glass. One of the gobblers was dominant and strutted at his reflection, flying up and striking out with his spurs every few minutes. The other one kept pace with him, pecking the glass. The less dominant one actually came up on the deck and looked me over very carefully from about ten feet. I sat there for about half an hour, hardly breathing or blinking an eye, and observed them closely.

In the sunlight their every feather gleamed iridescent blues and greens and the skin on their heads and necks was a bright

WILD TURKEY
Meleagris gallopavo

powder blue. They are very striking birds. Finally, Dorothy and a friend came into the greenhouse to get firewood, which alarmed them enough to cause both gobblers to gobble loudly; this in turn roused Tanner the puppy, who barked at them. This sent them running back into the woods to join the rest of the flock. I wasn't around Sunday afternoon, but Dorothy says that they were back to go another round with their reflections at about 4 PM.

A lot of tundra swans were going over the house Sunday evening as I worked around the yard. Three big flocks, about a thousand birds altogether, went arrowing due north, their wild cries echoing till they were out of sight. They will fly all night, coming down to feed Monday morning, a lot of them probably at Montezuma Wildlife Refuge in New York State.

Our red-bellied woodpeckers have excavated a nest hole in the top of a dead tulip poplar in the side yard. I can put my ear against the trunk and hear them tapping away inside the hole. Downy and pileated woodpeckers are using the same drumming station to drum out their territorial signals; the big pileated signals really echo through the woods.

18th April 1996

Our hummingbirds showed up the morning of April 13th this year. There were two of them, a male and female, and they hung around the feeder all morning. This is a late date for them, and probably explains why the female was present. Sunday evening I watched as a pair of males slowly hovered and helicoptered around one another. These posturings are all show and bluff: the combatants won't actually come to blows unless they are pretty well matched. One of them usually loses his nerve and retreats. If they are well matched they may come to an armed truce, both using the feeder but not at the same time.

Other migrant birds are arriving several weeks later this year as well. Saturday morning a blue-gray gnatcatcher became trapped in our greenhouse. These little birds resemble tiny mockingbirds and build nests almost as small as hummingbird nests. They are tame little birds, and this one perched on the end of a stick that I slowly extended to it and sat there as I carried it to a door and outside. Sunday morning I found a dead ovenbird on the deck. In spite of all our precautions, birds still try to take shortcuts through our sliding glass doors and a large percentage of them suffer broken necks.

The wild turkeys continue to pass through the edge of the woods several times a day. The two big gobblers and four jakes are the most consistent visitors. The hens come out for brief periods several times a day and scratch around in the leaves awhile before slipping away. I think that they are all sitting on clutches of eggs now, as they don't join the gobblers up in the top of the trees at roosting time.

9th May 1996

All of a sudden, overnight it seems, the character of the birdsong around the house in the mornings has changed considerably. Most noticeable are the lovely flute-like calls of the wood thrush. They are setting up territories and calling to warn other wood thrushes to stay out.

Both warbling and red-eyed vireos make their home in our deciduous wood, and both sing throughout the morning, the red-eyed in particular being a very persistent singer, calling all day from the tops of the tallest trees. Its nests, too, are usually placed in a small fork in the tops of the tallest deciduous trees. Our other nesting vireo, the white-eyed, is also present but is a skulker, its scolding call coming from dense thickets. It places its nests very low in these same dense thickets, usually within three feet of the ground.

We have at least one pair of summer tanagers in the woods around the yard. The male has a lovely song but as soon as I start to work around the yard he stops singing and scolds me persistently. Great-crested flycatchers call constantly from the woods around the yard and have begun to build a nest in one of the boxes I put up for them. Wood-pewees are around the yard too, but have not started to build yet.

One of our female hummingbirds has begun to make her nest somewhere along our driveway. I saw her collecting spider webs from the corner of our kitchen window Saturday morning then heading down the driveway.

Juncos and white-throated sparrows have finally left, and the only finch-type we have left are the chipping sparrows, towhees, cardinals—and the cowbirds of course. A brilliant blue male indigo bunting has been showing up at the feeder for the last several days, but neither he nor the chipping sparrows will nest around the house; both are hanging out along our driveway and will probably nest there, the indigo bunting in the grass and weeds along the ditch, and the chipping sparrows in the over-hanging pine limbs along one side of the driveway.

23rd May 1996

The wild turkeys are continuing to forage around the yard, three gobblers quite boldly, two hens very furtively. We haven't seen any poults with the hens here, but on Saturday I saw a hen sneak across Indian Trail Road and as I got close one lone poult about the size of a quail scooted across the road to join her. I stopped the car and could hear several "lost" calls peeping in the under-growth, so I hope this meant that she had more than one poult in her brood.

Adventures with Birds

OUT & ABOUT
IN THE COASTAL
PLAIN

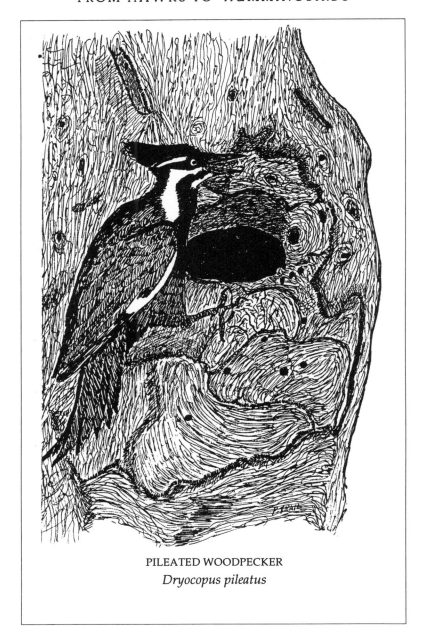

PILEATED WOODPECKER
Dryocopus pileatus

THE COASTAL PLAIN OF NORTH CAROLINA

abounds with back roads and country lanes that wind through swamps and woodlands and over many small bridges that span creeks and canals. These provide me with easy access to prime birding habitat. Traffic on most of them is light to non-existent and, since I use my car as a blind, they are perfect for my purposes. With an 800mm lens on my camera, mounted on a shoulder stock and resting on a bean bag on the car window, I can get large images of small birds from distances out to 100 feet. As long as I stay in the car I can move slowly and quietly without disturbing them. Apparently they see the car as a large harmless animal. Meanwhile, inside the car I have all the comforts of home—comfortable seat, food, and drink, binoculars, cameras, and bird books close at hand. I wait, and the birds come to me.

13th June 1985

Recently I spent the day on Pelican and Battery Islands in Cape Fear River off Southport. Robin Bjork, the Audubon Warden there, was doing research, and Mike Dunn, Regional Naturalist for North Carolina, and I were along to take photographs and observe the nesting pelicans, gulls, terns, ibis, egrets, and herons. It was a fabulous day, but when I returned I was covered to the waist with mud from the mud flats and salt marsh. Even after hosing down I still looked grubby and was pretty sure that most motels wouldn't let me in the door long enough to explain. What I should have done is found a motel first!

24th October 1985

Fall bird migration is well underway now. I see lots of redstarts and other fall warblers in the woods and flocks of robins passing through. Some of the robins will spend the winter with us, feeding on dogwood and other berries. The redstarts are easy to identify, but most fall warblers are listed in bird guides on pages entitled "Confusing Fall Warblers." The immatures of both sexes are a sort of grayish-brown, and the adult males and females, so clean and bright in the spring, have moulted their fancy feathers and are now clad in sombre hues. The result is that most of the species of wood warblers look pretty much alike and are hard to identify. The experienced birder uses habitat preferences, feeding patterns, flight characteristics, and other activities along with color patterns, and makes out fairly well, but the novice birder is usually hopelessly confused.

Incidentally, we consider the birds that nest in the United States as "our" birds, but most of them actually spend more time in the tropics than they do here. It always comes as a shock to me to see yellow warblers, probably the most common nesting warblers in New York State, flitting about in the tropical rain forest, and to see barn swallows along tropical rivers!

In a drive along Pea Island last weekend I saw hundreds of

migrating Cooper's and sharp-shinned hawks. A lot of them follow the coastline on their migrations, and the Outer Banks is a very good place to watch them on both the spring and fall migrations. These were flying very low over the bayberries and marsh grasses, hunting as they flew. Both these species are accipiters,* and their food is about 90 per cent small birds. I saw about a dozen kestrels or sparrow hawks, small colorful falcons who feed on mice and insects. I saw one merlin or pigeon hawk, a medium-sized falcon which feeds on small birds and shorebirds and is rather rare.

I also saw an adult peregrine falcon or duck hawk sitting on the ground feeding on a bird of some sort, probably a shorebird. It was on a section of road with soft sand along both sides and a lot of traffic, so we couldn't stop for a better look or to take photographs with the big telephoto lens. This large, powerful falcon takes smaller birds on the wing, but will stoop and knock larger birds (ducks and pigeons) out of the air and then land to feed on them on the ground. It is a great wanderer. I have seen one in Suriname capturing bats in the evening over the Suriname River and returning to a dead branch to feed. The bats only made a mouthful each; it caught and ate three while we watched, entranced. One of the fastest and most superb flyers in the bird world, it is an endangered species and had almost disappeared as a breeding species in the east. Captive breeding programs at Cornell University and other locations in the east, and the release of the young birds at selected sites in the wild, are slowly bringing it back. It is truly a magnificent bird, the epitome of power and grace, and to see one flying free is to get a glimpse of our lost wild America.

---

* woodland hawks: North America has three species—the sharp-shinned, the Cooper's, and the northern goshawk. Their long tails and short rounded wings give them great agility in their pursuit of songbirds, their principal prey.

FROM HAWKS TO HUMMINGBIRDS

7th November 1985

A week ago we left the house at about 8 AM to go to Nags Head Woods and be a part of their Tuesday volunteer work crew. We arrived late because the drawbridge over the Alligator River had become stuck in the open position and it took three hours to get it repaired and closed. We were in time to help clear the main trail of downed trees and branches. As we came out of the woods on the trail and entered a short section of sand dunes we saw a magnificent bald eagle, fully adult, with white head and tail, circling over Fresh Pond. In brilliant sunshine it circled slowly over our heads, quite low. It was worth the entire trip to see it.

21st November 1985

I had a frustrating experience on Sunday morning, trying to photograph a winter wren. My own fault, however. The proper technique for photographing birds from a car is to glide up to suitable habitat, cut off the motor, focus the lens approximately and set the lens aperture and shutter speed according to the light, then spish to attract the birds. A lot of small birds will come out of dense cover to see what's going on.

On this occasion I stopped beside a pile of downed trees overgrown with weeds and briars. I sat quietly for several minutes then began to spish—without getting the camera ready. A winter wren popped up very close, posed perfectly, while I tried frantically to get the camera in position. As I got it in perfect focus and was pressing the release, the wren popped down. Spishing again brought it out once more, but again it popped down before I could press the shutter release. I spished until I was blue in the face, but to no avail. Apparently, when that little wren heard one spish he'd heard them all and was no longer interested. I'll get photographs sooner or later—probably later, as the winter wren is almost as much mouse as bird: brown, very secretive, never still, skulking around on the ground under brushpiles. On its northern nesting grounds it is a superlative singer, but on migration it's silent and rarely seen.

I saw six turkey vultures Sunday morning, doing a most unvulture-like thing—eating peanuts! I wasn't sure what they were doing at first, so I watched them with binoculars for about twenty minutes. Two of them were perched on a huge roll of peanut hay and the other four were walking around like chickens, breaking peanut shells and eating the nuts.

We go every Wednesday to the Nature Conservancy's Nags Head Woods, where I'm helping with a Wildlife Watch and where in February I will be starting a breeding bird census. While getting acquainted with some of the terrain last week, I came upon a very interesting foraging band of birds. In winter small birds cease being territorial because they don't have young to raise, and they form foraging bands of many species. This particular band consisted of about six Carolina chickadees, probably a pair and their this year's offspring; yellow-rumped warblers; four brown creepers, very interesting little mousey birds who start at the base of a tree and spiral up around the trunk, probing crevices in the bark for insects; two downy woodpeckers; one yellow-bellied sapsucker; four red-breasted nuthatches, calling softly in their little "tin-flute" voices as they foraged among the pine-cone clusters in the tree tops; several pine warblers; and a ruby-crowned kinglet. All these birds feed in different niches and don't compete. They also benefit from more pairs of eyes watching for predators. They know and respond to each other's alarm calls, and they all froze when a Cooper's hawk came flying through the woods.

5th December 1985

Last week Mike Dunn drove up from Kinston and spent the day with me. I borrowed a canoe and we spent most of the day on Bennett Millpond. It's a beautiful pond, more open than Merchants Millpond at the state park in Gates County, and I think the water is a little deeper.

The shoreline has many coves with the water extending back into the cypress and tupelo trees. We glided silently into one of these and were able to get quite close to a red-tailed hawk sitting on a log and feeding on a muskrat. Canoeing always sets up a conflict for me. One the one hand it's so silent that you can sneak up quite close to all kinds of wildlife; on the other, I'm not an experienced canoeist and am reluctant to take my expensive camera equipment into the canoe with me. So we just looked and took no photographs.

We climbed up into one of the many duck-blinds to eat our lunch. From our perch we had a good look over the pond. There were about thirty ducks on the pond, mostly ringnecks, with a few mallards, baldpates, and gadwalls. Oh, and one coot, which allowed us to get quite close before pattering off. Back in the flooded coves we were able to spish up chickadees, white-breasted nuthatches, yellow-rumped warblers, red-bellied woodpeckers, downy woodpeckers, flickers, pileated woodpeckers, both golden-crowned and ruby-crowned kinglets, brown creepers, a phoebe, and both Carolina and winter wrens.

We paddled back towards the mill-house, exploring along the other side of the pond. The area along the east side of the pond is being logged, and I was sorry to see that several huge loblolly pines near the mill-house were gone. The pond and its flooded swamps are interesting places to explore during all the seasons. It has the only nesting record for the common merganser in North Carolina.

19th December 1985

Two weeks ago I spent Sunday at Lake Mattamuskeet. There were a lot of waterfowl close to the shore on the Route 94 causeway. It was a brilliant sunny day, and I took a lot of photographs using the car as a blind. swans, canvasbacks, ruddy ducks, ring-necked ducks, coots, and grebes were there in large numbers and allowed me to get quite close.

Later, Kelley Davis the wildlife biologist there took us on a drive along the dikes in the management area at the eastern end of the lake. During the two-hour tour we saw, at a conservative estimate, 40,000 swans, 30,000 blue and snow geese, and about 30,000 ducks of several species. There are quite a few raptors also, half a dozen marsh hawks, a like number of kestrels, and one immature bald eagle. Truly a remarkable number of birds and an unforgettable field trip.

I spent Saturday at Merchants Millpond State Park and in the area just west of Gatesville; there is a dirt road running for about six miles through some fairly large pine trees, where I'm hoping to see red-cockaded woodpeckers. I found a nest hole high up in a tall pine, but no sign of the actual woodpeckers. The dirt road and the numerous logging roads off it were full of pick-up trucks, deer hunters, and dogs, so I didn't do much hiking in the woods. Deer hunters always appear to be very serious about what they are doing, and I think they would regard a birder in their midst as a very frivolous intrusion indeed!

While it's still a little early for owls to be courting, both the barred and great horned owls seem to be becoming more vocal in my woods. I had quite a serenade for several nights last week. I've observed several screech-owls sitting in the entrance of their roosting holes, one quite low, allowing me to take a close-up photograph. If the great horned owl is considered the "flying tiger" of the woods at night, I think the screech-owl deserves the title "flying bobcat." While it takes mostly mice and rats, I have known it to take roosting birds up to flicker size—almost as large as the owl itself.

Altogether I've seen five screech-owls during the last three weeks, all gray-phase birds. For some reason, some screech-owls have red feathers instead of the more common gray, even in the same brood. In some areas of the south the red phase is the more common, but not apparently in our local area.*

3rd January 1986

The big red-tailed hawks who are very common around the countryside just now have started to pair up. They have always maintained a very loose pair bond but now have taken to perching close together in the same tree. The red-shouldered hawks are doing the same, but I haven't noticed any of their spectacular aerial courtship displays so far. Actually, most of the redtails we see here will migrate north in late February and nest in the northern US and Canada. I have seen them pass over the eastern end of Lake Ontario in the thousands in March and April. Two pairs nested in the big woods behind my house last year. One pair raised a single chick; I did not discover the other nest until just before the tree was felled during lumbering operations in November. I hope that pair will rebuild in my woods this coming year.

One of Richard Lichtenwalner's cats had a very unsettling experience with one of these big hawks last week. Richard had noticed a mouse in one of his feed bins and dropped a cat in to catch it. The cat caught it and carried it out into the yard to play with it for a while, as cats are wont to do. It would let the mouse run off a ways, pretending to ignore it, then suddenly pounce. What the cat didn't know was that a hungry redtail was watching from a tree across the road. When the mouse got about four feet from the cat, the hawk swooped down and neatly took the mouse from under the cat's nose, scaring the cat out of about two of its nine lives!

Logging operations are going on in the woods behind my house, and I go back once or twice a week to watch them. In the process of felling they often cut down trees that turn out to be hollow, and these hollow trees can turn out to be very interesting

---

* It never fails: the day after writing this I found a beautiful red-phase owl beside Route 17 just short of the Hertford interchange!

RED-TAILED HAWK
Buteo jamaicensis

to naturalists. A large tulip poplar, felled last week, had a large hollow in a crotch about forty feet up. It looked like an ideal nesting site for a horned owl or a barred owl, so I cleared out some of the dead wood debris from the felling operation and dug into the floor. It turned out to be quite interesting. At about three inches I began to find bones, which continued as far down as I dug, about a foot. No bird bones, but the skulls of gray and flying squirrels, parts of the lower jaws of what looked like small opossums, and leg bones of rabbits, squirrels, and other small animals. Judging by the depth of the deposits I estimate that owls had nested there for over thirty years.

6th February 1986

One of the things I got for Christmas was a five-yard long by five-feet high piece of camouflage netting. I have been devising ways to use this as a photographic blind to photograph birds. While the car is a pretty good and very comfortable blind, there are lots of places with birds where you can't drive a car. Last week I draped the net in the branches of a large fallen beech tree and was able to get good photographs of a covey of quail. There are about fifteen birds in this covey and I have been trying for months to get close-up photographs. In the woods where you can see them they are pretty spooky and won't let me get within fifty yards of them. Standing in my little blind hid me so effectively that they came within fifteen feet of me. My slow movements as I maneuvered the camera through a slit in the netting, and the clicking of the camera shutter, did not alarm them. As a matter of fact, after I had taken all the pictures I wanted I had to wait an extra half hour for them to move on out of sight before I could leave the blind! I want to use the netting this spring and summer in some of the fresh- and salt-water marshes to get photographs of rails and other marsh birds. I only hope the mesh is fine enough to keep out the hordes of mosquitoes!

I'm still hoping to get a good photograph of a winter wren.

Trying to photograph one is a very frustrating experience. Last Friday I drove down a farmer's lane to an old brushpile along the edge of the woods and was sitting in the car trying to spish out into the open a winter wren who had popped up once or twice. It finally disappeared for good and I was about to leave, when I glanced up at the edge of the woods and discovered an interested spectator. Sitting on the edge of a large hollow tree about forty feet away was a barred owl, very curious about all the spishing. I couldn't have posed it any better myself! In full sunlight, it sleepily kept an eye on me as I exposed half a roll of film, and it didn't move as I started the car and drove away.

20th February 1986

Remember the red-tailed hawk who had been hanging around Richard Lichtenwalner's barn, the one who robbed his cat of the mouse she had been playing with? Well, that hawk got into deep trouble last week and has now been deported from Chowan County!

It happened like this. I received a phone call from Richard about 6 pm on Thursday February 6th. A big hawk was in amongst his chickens inside the barn, and did I want it? I did, so I grabbed a long-handled minnow net, a canvas bag, and a pair of heavy gloves, and was at his barn in five minutes. I could hear the ruckus as soon as I opened the car door—all the hens were having royal hysterics. The hawk had entered the chicken house through a missing window pane that opened into the barn. What it was doing in the barn in the first place we don't know— probably after a rat.

Richard met me, we entered the barn and opened the door to the chicken house. There sitting on the top shelf was a very belligerent immature red-tailed hawk. Hens were rocketing around the room screaming bloody murder, and the hawk was totally confused. I quickly slapped the net over it, pulled it off the shelf, and pinned it to the floor. The hawk flopped over on its back and locked its formidable talons in the net. Since it refused to release its grip I was able to work a gloved hand under the net and grip both legs firmly, rendering it harmless. It has a powerful beak but made no attempt to use it. What it can do with its large talons, however, would be of technical interest to a bobcat: it is capable of sinking them completely through the palm of one's hand. Since it refused to release its grip, we stuffed hawk and net into the bag, tied the top, and I brought it home. At home I put a small black bag over its head. It immediately quieted down and I was able to persuade it to release its grip on the net so I could pop it into the big fiber barrel I keep for such purposes.

All hawks and owls are protected and cannot be shot or kept in one's possession, so I called Allan Elks of the NC Wildlife Resources Commission, who came over the next morning and took it off my hands. We discussed disposition and decided deportation out of the county was the best solution. It hasn't been back, so either it couldn't find its way back or the whole experience was so traumatic it didn't want to come back.

I saw a flock of about seventy cedar waxwings eating holly berries in one of the large holly trees across Broad Street from the Court House. Waxwings have been known to get drunk from eating too many berries and to act very silly.

6th March 1986

These longer days are arousing the amorous instincts of the red-shouldered hawks. On the way to the mailbox last week I heard a pair screaming overhead, up very high. While I watched them soaring in circles, the male suddenly dropped like a rock for several hundred feet. Screaming like a banshee, he pulled out of his dive with a barrel roll and rode a thermal up to repeat the performance. I'm keeping my eyes open for their nest back in the woods behind the house.

20th March 1986

I have mixed feelings about our two species of accipiters, the sharp-shinned and Cooper's hawks. I don't like them to haunt my bird feeder and catch birds there three or four times a day; on the other hand I really admire the consummate skill and dash they show when they are hunting.

Last week I was driving south on Route 32 out of Edenton when a male sharpshin came low across the road in front of me, flew at top speed up Jackson Street at about a foot above the ground, and snatched a junco from a flock feeding in the grass on the right side of the street. Without stopping, he hedge-hopped across a back yard and landed in the trees over by the old silo. Then, the other morning as I was driving down my driveway, I flushed a Cooper's hawk from a tree at the edge of the woods. She pitched down low across the driveway in front of me and into a deep drainage ditch running at right angles to the driveway. I stopped and watched as she flew at top speed down the ditch for several hundred yards below the level of the banks on each side.

Last week I had a ringside seat as another superb aerial hunter performed. I had driven out to Drummond Point and parked the car, got out, and was watching several bluebirds through the binoculars when they abruptly dashed into the protection of a fallen cedar tree. I looked around and saw a merlin flying low along the bank of the Albemarle Sound. A little way past me it flew over a narrow strip of broomsedge and put up a mixed flock of small birds including several flickers and about a dozen meadowlarks. With several quick flaps of its wings it accelerated and stooped at a flicker. It moved so fast that it appeared the flicker was standing still. The flicker is a large bird, and at the last minute the merlin veered off, pulled up, came around, and accelerated swiftly after a meadowlark. It hit the meadowlark in a puff of feathers, bound on, and came to earth in the broom-sedge. It didn't fly up, so it was apparently plucking the meadow-lark and feeding on the ground.

26th March 1986

This spring sees the start of the breeding bird census for North Carolina. A lot of preliminary work has already gone into the project. The entire state has been divided into one-mile-square blocks. These small blocks have been consolidated into larger blocks (five blocks wide and five deep) of twenty-five square miles each. These large blocks have been numbered and are available to interested birders who might like to drive and walk through them this spring and summer, observing and making a list of all the bird species that are breeding.

I have been given three such blocks: one centered on Valhalla, one with my house in the center, and the adjacent block to the east which centers roughly on Nixon's Beach and runs to the Yeopim River. I drive and walk through these areas a lot anyway, and it isn't as much work as it sounds. I don't have to walk over every square foot of it, but just have to make sure I cover all the habitat types in each block. It's healthy work, you're outdoors a lot, and do a lot of sitting quietly watching what goes on in the woods, fields, and swamps.

The project may take four or five years to complete, and when it is finished the information will be fed into computers and eventually a Breeding Bird Atlas* for North Carolina will be published.

3rd April 1986

I observed and photographed two red-cockaded woodpeckers last week. I have been trying to locate these birds for more than a year. This little woodpecker is a southern species and is now on the endangered species list because it requires extensive stands of old, large, long-leaf or loblolly pines. It can forage in smaller, younger pines, but requires the old pines for excavating nest holes.

---

* At the time of publication, the Atlas had not yet been published.

ADVENTURES WITH BIRDS

I had taken part in an Audubon Christmas Bird Count at Goose Creek State Park last year and when I received a summary of all the birds seen I noticed three red-cockaded woodpeckers on the list. All three birds had been seen by James and Mary McLaurin at their bird feeder. I called the McLaurins, who invited us to visit them at their home just outside Bath. We spent a very interesting and enjoyable half day there last Thursday. In addition to the woodpeckers, there were a lot of other birds in the grounds around the house. We got a quick glimpse of a brown-headed nuthatch and discovered an early nesting brown thrasher in a bush in the yard. If one was quiet, several bobwhite quail would approach and scratch busily in the leaves almost at one's feet. The woodpeckers were life birds* for me. I can tell you, after birding actively for over forty years life birds in North America do not come along too often. All in all, a delightful visit.

The weather Saturday morning was so nice that Harry Lassiter and I took his boat and went fishing along the shoreline from the Chowan River Bridge to Edenton Bay. In a a one-mile stretch along the shore are four active osprey nests. The first one is enormous, about five feet high and a local landmark for over twenty years. It has spawned two satellite nests about a quarter of a mile apart that have been in use for several years. At the end of the line a pair of ospreys are in the process of building the fourth nest. This must be their first attempt, as they have selected a side limb of a cypress instead of a more secure and stable location in the top of the tree.

While we fished we could watch them collecting and adding sticks to the nest. Their methods of nest building were interesting. They would fly at a small branch in the top of a dead tree and hit it hard enough with their feet to break off a two- or three-foot section, which would be carried back to the nest, where the

* so called when a particular species is seen for the first time in one's life

female would fussily tuck-fit it in until she was satisfied. The female collected a hanging clump of Spanish moss the same way and carried it back to the nest in triumph, with the smaller male flying alongside and whistling encouragement. It's great to see the osprey population recovering and repopulating the shoreline.

10th July 1986

Last week, driving down the long driveway to Somerset Farm, I came upon three baby killdeers running before the car. I stopped the car, grabbed the camera, and ran down the last one in line. It darted into the grass beside the road and squatted motionless and unblinking while I took several photographs at very close range. It was about a day old, a downy gray and white bit of fluff, with long pink legs, big feet, and knobby knees: an enchanting little creature. When I returned half an hour later the frantic parents had coaxed all three of them across a ditch and out into a bean field.

I had a somewhat similar experience two days later with a newly hatched brood of quail. I had parked the car and walked a few steps into the woods, when I flushed a hen quail, who flopped across the ground in a distraction display. I froze immediately and found myself in the midst of a peeping brood of at least a dozen baby quail about the size of bumblebees. The mother gave a warning cluck and the babies all fell silent and hid. One second there were a dozen little mites running around my feet, and the next they had all vanished. They were so tiny, and there were so many, that I was afraid that if I kneeled to find one to photograph I might accidentally crush several. So I very carefully backed out and sat quietly in the car. In a few minutes the mother gave her gathering call, and the place where I had been standing came alive as the tiny brown forms scurried across the path and into the woods.

7th August 1986

While driving out to Drummond Point on Sunday morning just

after a heavy rain, I rounded a curve and came upon a flock of eleven wild turkeys standing in the road. I stopped the car about four hundred yards away, took several photographs with the telephoto lens, and observed them for several minutes through the binoculars. There were five poults about half grown, three hens, and three larger birds, probably gobblers. I drove slowly towards them and they eased into the woods. I drove on down to Drummond Point, turned around, and had driven back about a mile when I saw a turkey along the edge of a weedy field. I stopped the car and, as I watched, four more came out of the weeds, following the first one. Three of these were gobblers with long beards, and one of them was huge. The last two were hens. They strolled along the edge of the weeds until a heavy rumble of thunder sounded, whereupon they all speeded up and ducked back into the weeds.

This is part of a flock of wild turkeys trapped on Camp Lejeune and released in this area two years ago. It's good to see that they are now reproducing. With landowners and hunters cooperating, it's hoped that they will spread to other suitable areas as their population grows.

18th September 1986

Sunday night, as I listened to the Navy Brass Quintet on the Old Courthouse Green, I watched as about three hundred chimney swifts swirled around the courthouse chimney and by the dozen began to drop fluttering into it. In about fifteen minutes all were safely roosting in it for the night. These are probably northern US or Canadian chimney swifts, and in the morning they will resume their migration, feeding on the wing as they go.

2nd October 1986

A few kestrels are back to spend winter with us, and I've seen several marsh hawks tilting over harvested cornfields. The next several months should be excellent for observing the fall hawk migration along the Outer Banks, especially along Pea Island.

FROM HAWKS TO HUMMINGBIRDS

20th November 1986

Sunday evening at about dusk, as I was leaving the wooded section of Country Road 1203, I saw a great horned owl alight on a stub of a dead hickory in the field beside the road. I stopped the car and watched as the owl swiveled its head around to face us, showing his feathered "horns." It looked over the field for a minute, then swooped low across the field and, with several swift wing strokes, vanished into the darkening woods. This is a big, powerful owl, the supreme aerial night-time predator over all of North, Central, and South America. To experience the essence of wild America one should be in the woods at night, alone, not a sound of civilization anywhere, then have the deep menacing hoots of this owl sound from the woods somewhere behind you!

1st January 1987

We spent Saturday at the Mattamuskeet National Wildlife Refuge and had an interesting day. We saw two bald eagles, an adult and an all-brown immature. We got a very good look and good pictures of a troop of brown-headed nuthatches. The birds had a favorite crevice in the stub of a broken pine limb and took turns wedging pine seeds in it and then cracking them open with hammer blows of the beaks to get at the kernel inside. This is close to the northern limit of their range, and I was glad to get photographs of them. These tiny energetic foragers were life birds for my daughter Robin and her husband Joe, who were with me.

29th January 1987

I got a call last week from Barnard Patterson out on Country Club Drive. He had a large hawk in his back yard which had been hanging around for several days. I drove over to get a look at it and we were able to observe it for quite a while. It was an immature red-shouldered hawk and it was feeding on earthworms which had been forced to the surface by the recent heavy rains. What surprised me was its tameness. It was making free with several back yards, landing very close to houses. It wasn't paying too much attention to the blue jays which were scolding it, and only flew back into the woods when several dogs rushed at it.

12th February 1987

I've been watching a flock of about four hundred Canada geese out on Drummond Point for the last several days. I'll take my Celestron telescope out there this week to see if any of the geese are wearing colored neck bands. New York and Maryland as well as North Carolina are neck-banding geese, and it will be interesting to see if the recent heavy snows further north have pushed some of the "shortstoppers" on down to North Carolina. In the cut-over area just short of Drummond Point I found a pair of red-headed woodpeckers and got close enough to get several photographs with the big telephoto lens. It's ideal habitat for them, and I hope they nest there this spring.

26th February 1987

Sunday morning I saw the largest flock of cedar waxwings that I have ever seen. I had just dropped Dorothy off at the Methodist church, and as I left the parking lot I saw an enormous flock of them wheeling over the former Ward estate across the road and field from the church. I drove over, parked at the site of the Farmer's Market, and watched and took photographs for about two hours.

The birds were resting in the tops of cypress and oak trees and every twenty minutes or so would fly down into several of the big cedar trees and feast on the powder-blue cedar berries. Actually, it was more of a feeding frenzy than feast: they would hang from a branch by the hundreds, some upside down, and gobble berries frantically. At the height of the activity I estimate that there were over two thousand birds present. Small flocks of thirty to a hundred were constantly leaving and heading north, while other flocks were dropping from high in the sky to the south and joining those resting in the trees and feeding. During the two hours observation I estimate that I saw over four thousand cedar waxwings.

Shortly after I left, it started to rain, and the rain lasted all afternoon and into the night. There had also been a constant trickle of grackles and red-wing blackbirds going over, headed north, so I suspect that waxwings, grackles, and blackbirds were all going north just ahead of the weather front. As far as I could tell there were no bohemian waxwings among them. I took half a roll of color slides and I shall check these carefully for bohemians. When there are so many birds present, all moving, and you're trying to get a sharp focus through a telephoto lens, it is hard to spot minor size and plumage differences.

3rd April 1987

The pair of red-headed woodpeckers that I have been observing all winter in the cut-over woods on Drummond Point are finally digging a nest hole. They are being pestered continuously by Starlings, who sometimes drive them from the nest holes when they have them completed. There is a new mockingbird nest in the big vitex bush in the garden of the Cupola House. It has four very young nestlings in it and, as it is very close to the sidewalk, if you stand quietly you can watch the parents feed them from a very close distance.

21st May 1987

My work on the Breeding Bird Atlas for North Carolina is coming along quite well. In my three blocks I have confirmed seventy species of birds as breeding here, and the list is growing, albeitmore slowly now. Some interesting facts are coming to light. The brown-headed cowbird, for instance, is turning out to be a serious nest predator among some of the warblers and smaller birds.

In a nest of a common yellowthroat I found two cowbird and no yellowthroat fledglings. The two cowbird fledglings overflowed the small nest and were about twice the size of the hard-working foster parents. Earlier had I found the nest of an iindigo bunting with two cowbird eggs and no bunting eggs. Then, two weeks ago along a logging road I noticed a female prairie warbler carrying nesting material, and by sitting down in the road and observing for half an hour I was able to locate the nest in a small shrub. I left without approaching the nest and returned last Saturday to get photographs with the telephoto lens. Both birds had been very active around the nest site while building, and after waiting half an hour or so and seeing no sign of them, I carefully investigated the nest. Inside I found a cowbird egg and no warbler eggs. I checked it again two days later and found the situation unchanged. Apparently the warblers have abandoned the nest. I will check again in three days, and if there is no change I will collect the nest and egg for the Nature Conservancy. It is a beautifully crafted nest with a deep cup, made with fine grasses, willow cotton, and spiderwebs.

The female cowbird is a very sneaky operator who builds no nest of her own. She watches quietly until she locates the nest of a small bird; then, very early in the morning while the owners are absent, she slips in and lays an egg. If the owners already have an egg in the nest she may remove it. She may come back the next morning and lay another egg. Several days later she locates another nest and lays several eggs in it. During the season she may lay as many as twenty eggs, parasitizing half a dozen small birds. Some species will accept the cowbird eggs, and hatch and raise the young, as the yellowthroats were doing; some will abandon the nest, as the prairie parblers did; some will remove the cowbird eggs; and some will build a floor over the cowbird eggs. Yellow warbler nests have been found with as many as four floors, each covering cowbird eggs. However, enough birds are duped and raise the cowbirds as their own to make this a viable reproduction scheme for the cowbirds.

In pursuit of the breeding bird census I have been following the bulldozer which is working on the new nine holes for the local golf course. Two of the new holes will be across Airport Road in a swampy area which was logged two years ago. I have found nine nesting species during the clearing operation.

2nd July 1987

Our new neighbors, Dave and Virginia Crowell, are in the midst of moving from Rhode Island to their new home on Route 32 South; we stopped by to see them for a few minutes on Sunday evening. While we were admiring the view from the back porch, a female blue grosbeak flew by with a piece of paper larger than herself. She landed in a low spot behind the house, the site of a future pond, and flitted about in the grass and brush for several minutes before finally dropping the paper and gathering several green stems. She is nest-building somewhere nearby and Dave and Virginia are keeping an eye on her to try to locate the nest for me. This bird has the habit of using the shed skin of a snake in its nest, and I suspect she though the paper was a snake skin.

7th July 1987

A week or so ago I visited the SPCA shelter to look over the puppies. Someone had left a box there with three young chimney swifts in it. The best way to handle baby chimney swifts when they fall down your chimney is to put them back into the chimney. They have very strong feet and spikes on their tail feathers and can climb back up the chimney, where the parents will continue to feed them. They are difficult to raise, but I took these three home. Two of them have survived and are almost ready to fly. I am kept busy finding grasshoppers for them and will be glad when they are on their own. As soon as they can fly I'll find some kind soul who already has chimney swifts in their chimney, and release these two into the chimney with the others.

10th September 1987

I got a call last week from Larry McClure near Cypress Point

Marina. He has three hummingbird feeders and upwards of thirty hummingbirds using them. He reported that he had a white hummingbird coming to one of his feeders in the evenings. Because of the time of arrival, about 7:30 PM, I suspected that it might be a hawkmoth instead of a hummingbird. These large moths fly like hummingbirds and sometimes are attracted to the sugar water in feeders.

I went to his house on Friday evening and found that it was in fact a very light gray hummingbird. It was too dark to get photographs, so I went back on Saturday morning and spent three house waiting in vain for it to show up. I went out again on Sunday morning, and after about one hour it showed up and I was able to get photographs. It's an odd little bird, but not an albino. Feet, eyes, and beak are dark, and it has a few dark spots on its wings. It's smaller than the other hummingbirds, has no tail feathers, and its upper tail coverts form a short half circle on its rump. It's just as feisty and combative as the rest of the breed, hardly staying still long enough to photograph.

8th October 1987

The recent cold front that moved in and is still hanging around should push down a wave of migrating birds. Sparrows, finches, and juncos need a little snow in the north country to push them along. I saw a large flock of tree swallows across the road from the airport on Sunday morning. They had probably been flying all night, were hungry, and, since the cold snap had grounded small flying insects, several hundred of them were busy eating berries from a clump of wax myrtle bushes.

29th October 1987

My son Pepper, a professional ornithologist, probably has over a thousand bird species on his life list, but he did not have a red-cockaded woodpecker. I knew of the area west of Gatesville with a thin strand of big pines along each side of a dirt road, a suitable habitat for red-cockaded woodpeckers, so on Tuesday

SNOW GOOSE
Chen caerulescens

afternoon we drove over and hiked along the road.

It was a pleasant day and a very interesting area. We found several large Io moth caterpillars feeding on young persimmon plants, and watched a band of brown-headed nuthatches foraging among the pine cones. They found a crack in a pine stub and took turns wedging pine seeds into it then cracking them with vigorous blows of their beaks, calling continuously with little soft toots. A tame, fearless little bird, very interesting to observe.

We first heard, then saw, a red-cockaded woodpecker high in a big pine. It was quite wary and flew back into the woods after a minute or so, and although we heard it again we could not locate it. They are colony nesters and stay in the home range all year, so I shall go back later and try to determine the size of the colony. The road is rather deserted, and as long as the pines remain uncut I think they will stay in the area. It is not so much the presence of people that causes their disappearance but the loss of habitat, and their habitat is shrinking every year.

19th November 1987

We spent several days last week birdwatching on Pea Island with friends from New York State. Small numbers of Canada geese, snow geese, and tundra swans are early arrivals, and there are fair numbers of shorebirds, herons, ibis, and egrets. The main push of ducks, swans, and geese will be later when snow begins to cover the ground up north. We got a very close look at a common but rarely seen bird and a good look at a very rare one.

The first was an American bittern. This large wading bird is common in marshes but prefers to remain in the deep reed beds, rarely venturing out to the edges except to feed. We found one in a small pool which was surrounded by a dense growth of wax myrtles. Upon sighting us it slipped out of the shallow water and into the grass and weeds, where it froze motionless, bill pointing straight up. It blended so perfectly with the background that if you took your eyes off of it for a second and then looked back it took a minute to find it again. It was very unusual to get such a close look at one, and I took a series of color photographs of it. Walking along a nature trail a little later I met Kent Turner of the National Park Service and was introduced to a group of BBC cameramen who were shooting footage for a nature series to be shown on PBS TV in about two years. I told them about the bittern and found out that they had seen and photographed it earlier.

The really rare bird was an adult peregrine falcon. It was sitting on the cross-arm of a telephone pole when I got a glimpse of it as we drove by. We turned around and drove back on the shoulder of the road, stopped almost directly opposite, and observed it for about ten minutes. The peregrine is a big falcon, heavy-shouldered and wedge-shaped, with a distinctive black wedge extending below its eye. Three noisy fish crows on the next pole attracted its attention. It took off, made a preliminary pass at them and, when they took flight, came around, accelerated, and almost caught one as they suddenly realized their danger and dived into the bayberry bushes. It then flew along the edges of the marsh, putting up shorebirds, ducks, and gulls, before finally disappearing across the marsh.

10th December 1987

I spent half a day at Lake Mattamuskeet last week. There are a lot of tundra swans on the lake, three or four rafts of coots of about 5,000 each, scattered ducks of about six species, and at least three bald eagles, one an adult with white head and tail. One lone osprey was still hanging around near the causeway.

24th December 1987

Our winter quota of kestrels, or sparrow hawks, are with us. Every mile of power line has three or four of these graceful little falcons, who hunt mice along the grassy ditches. Big marsh hawks with prominent white rumps are busy quartering almost every large harvested field and its ditches. They too are after mice but also take any unwary ground-feeding birds. They are constantly flushing meadowlarks out of the tall grass.

21st January 1988

Matt and I got a good look at three adult bald eagles last week. We were traveling east down Indian Trail Road, and about half a mile past St John's Church we saw a very large bird swing across the road and into a thermal. I stopped the car and we got out and put the binoculars on it. It was an eagle, about five years old, with a pure white tail and a head and neck that were almost all white. It continued to circle over our heads as it rode the thermal upwards. I took several photographs of it as it rose higher and finally topped out and headed east towards Drummond Point. There are two new osprey nests on the point, and this might be an area in which an eagle would hang out. We drove to the point and looked along the shore with binoculars: a flock of Canada geese were in the field but there was nothing around the osprey nests or along the shore.

We birded for a while, and as we started to get back in the car Matt looked up—there were two adult bald eagles wheeling in tight circles above us. It resembled a courtship flight, and at times the two were so close that I got several photographs with both eagles in the same frame. They headed west along the northern shore of the Sound and roughly over Greenfield were joined by a third eagle, which we believe was the one we had sighted previously. They dropped lower and may have landed along the shore between Greenfield and the Sound Bridge. There are several osprey nests along this stretch of shoreline, and eagles are attracted to them as places to perch. As a matter of fact, eagles will also take over an osprey nest, add to it, and nest there themselves. The northern shore of Albemarle Sound, fairly isolated, has quite a few osprey nests already, with new ones being added each year. With the bald eagle population slowly rising I think it's only a question of time before we have one or two nesting pairs of bald eagles as well.

Sunday morning I saw a marsh hawk or harrier catch a hispid rat on a ditch bank along Route 32 South. It landed in a grassy field about fifty yards from the road and, for once, allowed the car to stop opposite it without flying off. I focused the 800 mm telephoto lens on it and took several photographs as well as observing it. It settled down to feed hungrily and soon attracted several panhandlers. The first was a crow which landed close by and looked longingly at the feast but didn't dare get too close. When the crow left, a kestrel came over and dive-bombed the harrier several times, protesting its intrusion into its hunting territory. As I continued to watch through the viewfinder the harrier suddenly took flight with the remainder of the rat in its talons, and a big red-tailed hawk flashed through the viewfinder field and set off in hot pursuit. The redtail is a bigger hawk, and if it could have surprised the harrier it would have robbed it of its prey.

4th February 1988

I attended the Carolina Bird Club winter meeting in Nags Head last week, spending all day Saturday birding from Whalebone Junction to Ocracoke Island. A lot of the time was spent in learning some of the finer points of gull identification. Most gulls take four years to reach maturity, so they have four different juvenile plumages plus the breeding plumage and the adult winter plumage. In the winter you have all the various ages and plumages, except the breeding plumage, mixed together for at least three species, so trying to identify precisely what you're looking at is a bit tricky at times. The weather was beautiful, the ocean almost as calm as a millpond, and the group I was with saw about fifty thousand gulls, all of the most common species: ring-billed, herring, and great black-backed. Other groups added four more gull species: laughing, little, Bonaparte, and lesser black-backed. The lesser black-backed and the little gulls are European species which are rare along the east coast.

We saw at least ten thousand northern gannets resting on the water just offshore, and at one point just north of Avon saw about four hundred of them feeding . They are big white birds with black wing-tips, and they closed their wings and dived into the ocean from about a hundred feet up, disappearing into the water like feathered javelins with hardly a splash, a magnificent sight to watch. We looked for, but did not find, common eider and king eider ducks and a harlequin duck which had been seen in Oregon Inlet earlier, but did find a Eurasian wigeon in the Bodie Island Lighthouse pond. It's similar to our green-winged teal but is a very rare duck in North America. Saturday night after dinner all the groups met and compared notes. Altogether we had observed a total of 159 species of birds for the day.

Sunday morning was so warm and spring-like that I spent most of it out near the Edenton Airport trying to get close-up photographs of a meadowlark. I didn't have much luck with the meadowlark, but did get several close-ups of a killdeer which was pulling out earthworms like a robin and came quite close to the car in the process.

On the other side of the car was a large overgrown clump of privet. It was tree size and loaded with dark berries. A mockingbird had staked a claim to it and was vigorously driving away any other birds who came to feed. While I was watching, it chased away a robin, a catbird, three blue jays, and when a flock of a dozen cedar waxwings landed to feed, it attacked each one individually and eventually chased the entire flock across the road!

It's still a little early, but I noticed several pairs of bluebirds investigating nest holes in a logged-over area near Drummond Point. They have not shown any interest in my nest boxes as yet, however. I also observed a pair of brown-headed nuthatches going through courtship activities.

18th February 1988

About this time every year small flocks of cedar waxwings seem to come together and form quite large flocks. Three hundred to a thousand birds will settle in the top of a large tree and stay there most of the day, splitting up into smaller flocks at intervals to feed, but coming back and rejoining the main flock to rest.

During Friday, Saturday, and Sunday last week just such a large flock was centered in the big trees around St Paul's Church. Smaller flocks of fifty to a hundred birds would leave the main flock and descend upon the holly trees along the business district. Traffic and pedestrians kept them in constant motion, but they were rapidly stripping the trees of berries. Cedar waxwings are very partial to the fruits of holly, dogwood, hawthorn, and crab apple, and will stay in an area until all the fruits are gone before moving on.

Their feeding behavior is very odd. A flock will sit quietly preening for half and hour or so, then, almost as one, about half the birds will descend on a food tree and for several minutes the tree will seethe with them like sharks in a feeding frenzy. Then back to the resting tree they fly to sit quietly with the rest of the flock. As they move north as spring advances, the large flocks will gradually break up until there are only pairs on the nesting grounds.

3rd March 1988

Small flocks of wood ducks are appearing in flooded areas along the roads and I've been attempting to get photographs. There aren't many birds prettier than a wood drake in courting plumage. But, I'll tell you, I'm having a lot of problems: plastic bags, pop bottles, foam hamburger containers, plastic cups—you name it, it's there. A beautiful duck, focused and framed, and in the background what appears to be a public dump! I've never seen anyone throw trash from a car, but it's there, somebody does it. I wonder who, but most of all, I wonder *why?*

21st April 1988

Birds sometimes pick the oddest places to nest. Two years ago a Carolina wren built her nest in a dog-food bag full of cedar shavings for our dog's bed; last year she built it in a very busty half torso piece of stoneware sculpture on the deck; this year she put the nest in a stack of flower pots in the storage shed. A pair of rough-winged swallows are nesting in a section of drain tile eroding out of the Albemarle Sound bank at Drummond Point. In the gravel along the edge of the road at Drummond Point two pair of killdeer have scratched out hollows, lined them with gravel, and will be laying eggs in them in a few days.

I am particularly observant of nesting birds just now as I am still working on the state's Breeding Bird Atlas Project. This entails a lot of quiet observing in a lot of wild places and, since birds are mainly creatures of edges, a lot of quiet observation in quite civilized places as well.

In line with this, I spent an hour on Sunday morning in Harry and Marginette Lassiter's yard. They have a bluebird box that's occupied, and in addition I found a robin's nest in the magnolia tree, a downy woodpecker nest in a dead limb of a sweet gum tree, and a mourning dove nest with two eggs in it in the hedgerow. Harry has driven a number of two-inch diameter pipes into his garden to make posts to hold grapevines. I observed a Carolina chickadee landing on one of these posts then disappearing down the open top. I got a stepladder and shone a flashlight down the inside. There, about twenty inches from the top, sat the chickadee on her nest, glaring back at me. Her body filled the interior diameter, head and tail jammed against opposite sides and both pointing straight up! Since chickadees usually lay four to six eggs, it's going to get very claustrophobic in that pipe when the eggs hatch and the young get some size on them, to say nothing of the parents climbing up and down twenty inches of vertical pipe hundreds of times a day to feed the hungry brood!

The surprises were not over yet. A pair of brown-headed nut-hatches, a strictly southern species—hole nesters, usually found in pine forests—lit in the pecan tree overhead. Calling softly to each other, they worked their way along a big branch, then down to the grapevines. They went along the top wire and when they reached the iron pipe post at the end the female promptly dived into its open top. The male sat quietly for several minutes then flew into the hedgerow. He was back in a few minutes with a piece of dried grass which he handed down into the pipe to the female. This is a very feisty little bird, never still for a moment, that I have been wanting to photograph for a long time. I un-limbered the big telephoto lens and got several shots while the male was transferring nesting material. Later, when they both left, I took a quick look down the pipe with a flashlight: they have a neat little nest about ten inches down the pipe.

15th Septeember 1988

This fall I'm collecting fresh-killed birds from under the TV tower and the FM radio tower near Columbia. The TV tower rises 1000 feet, the FM tower 660 feet. Birds migrate at night, and during foggy or rainy weather they fly into the towers and the guy wires supporting them. The birds I collect go to David Lee, Curator of Birds at the NC Museum of Natural Science, who prepares study skins for the museum. Last week I collected six bobolinks, two unidentified warblers, and a slim, long-legged, delicate little solitary sandpiper.

Under the TV tower I found a live American bittern. It had a broken wing and was quite belligerent. I wrapped it carefully in a pillowcase, brought it home, and placed it in a barrel in the greenhouse, fully expecting it to be dead the next morning. It is a very beautiful cryptically marked bird of brown and tan stripes. When I opened the barrel the next morning it had arranged itself in a fluffy mound of striped feathers, with its long neck, pointed beak, and glaring yellow eyes arising out of the middle pointing directly at my nose. I called David Rowe, District Wildlife biologist, and arranged for him to pick it up and take it to Amy Brown in Ahoskie. She runs a Wildlife Rehabilitation Center, mostly for raptors, and might be able to repair the bittern and release it.

Almost any fine evening this month, if you look up over downtown Edenton you will see a lot of migrating chimney swifts. Swifts feed on the wing and high up, so they migrate during daylight hours. Come evening, they look for large chimneys to roost in during the night and, as downtown Edenton has a lot of such chimneys, we host a lot of chimney swifts during their fall and spring migrations. Last Monday several hundred were pouring down the chimney at the old Swain School building.

27th October 1988

The series of long inter-connected ponds that run from the Pelikan Plant across Highway 32 and along Village Creek almost to Queen Anne's Creek is very attractive to herons, egrets, and, in the winter, ducks and geese. Last Wednesday I parked the car near the middle pond and was photographing a small flock of cattle egrets when my attention was attracted by a large raptor diving repeatedly at something on the ground beyond a screen of dog fennel at the edge of a peanut field, about five hundred yards away. Through the binoculars I identified it as a peregrine falcon, and it was actively harassing something on the ground. I quickly drove to Highway 32 then down the driveway leading to the Pelikan Company. When I got to within a hundred yards I turned the car broadside and reached for the camera. The raptor on the ground was a red-tailed hawk and it was mantling a grey item, a bird about the size of a pigeon.

As I was carefully lining up the camera with its 800 mm lens, the peregrine came in fast and low and actually hit the rump of the redtail with its feet. The redtail flopped on its back defensively for a second then abandoned the kill and headed for the woods across the field. The peregrine swooped up and around and stooped at the redtail again, grazing it lightly and knocking loose a small puff of feathers. The redtail made the safety of the woods, and the peregrine swung back and landed on the kill. All during its stooping attacks the peregrine was very vocal, uttering its loud rasping calls. I steadied the camera on it and took about a dozen photographs as it began to pluck the kill and feed ravenously. The kill was a small gull, most probably a laughing gull.

As I was attempting to get a little closer, a pick-up truck swung around me and drove rapidly down the edge of the field, putting the peregrine to flight. It took the gull with it, struggling to lift it, and gained enough altitude to clear the hedgerow at the end of the field. It then dropped down into another field and I was unable to observe it further. I examined the kill site and found two circles of gull feathers about six feet apart. In the larger circle of gull feathers I found several rump feathers from the redtail and a leg of the gull with the knee joint intact.

From looking at the evidence, I think that the peregrine knocked the gull out of the air but did not bind on, which explains the smaller circle of back and neck gull feathers. The redtail then left its perch on a nearby utility pole and completed the kill, judging by the larger circle of gull feathers and evidence of a struggle in the sandy soil. The peregrine, swinging back after hitting the gull, found the redtail in possession and began stooping on it, eventually hitting it and driving it into the woods before coming back to feed.

10th November 1988

Last week along the south side of Lake Phelps, while attempting to spish a catbird out into the open, I attracted a bird I was not expecting to see. A brightly marked white-crowned sparrow popped out of the brush and sat quietly about fifteen feet away, long enough for me to take several photographs. That area will be in our Christmas Count area, so I hope it sticks around.

The kestrels who spend the winter with us are back. I can count about half a dozen on the power lines along Highway 32 from my driveway to the Edenton town limits.

Last Friday afternoon out on Sandy Point I spent about an hour in the middle of the largest concentration of robins that I have ever seen. When I arrived there were already a lot of them feeding on Virginia creeper berries in the overgrown fields on the east side of the road, and more were arriving all the time. Using the binoculars I could see large numbers of robins flying out of the north east at about 1,200 feet. As they neared the north shore of Albemarle Sound, most of them turned back and dived for the woods. At times the sky literally rained robins as they closed their wings and dropped like stones. Clouds of them left the woods and drifted like leaves across the road into a peanut field. The woods for about a quarter mile along the road were seething with robins, and the field opposite was covered with them. At the height of the concentration I estimate that there were at least ten thousand robins present.

There were a few flocks of red-wing blackbirds and several small flocks of cedar waxwings as well. The robins were flying unusually high, and individuals were scattered out, not in tight flocks like blackbirds and grackles. Apparently they had been riding a front out of the north east all day and dropped down along the north shore of the Sound to feed and rest. While I was there, several thousand left in a scattered wave, climbing back to about a thousand feet and heading south west across the Sound. When I left, the woods and field were still full of robins and a few were still dropping out of the sky.

15th December 1988

Sunday morning was a pretty raw cold day. I spent most of the morning trying to get close-up photographs of meadowlarks. Most meadowlarks are pretty skittish, but I found a flock along

Montpelier Drive in Edenton that let me get fairly close. I took several shots but still haven't got the photographs I want.

2nd March 1989

All the way into town on Sunday morning there were lots of birds along the road where the snowplow had cleared the snow from the road shoulders, but there was too much traffic to take photographs. Late Sunday morning I drove out toward Rocky Hock, and right where Rocky Hock Landing Road intersects Highway 32 I ran into an enormous flock of cedar waxwings and robins. There are several big red cedars along the side of the road and a large grove of them around a house just off the road. A thousand or so cedar waxwings and several hundred robins were feeding on the cedar berries. I found a place where I could get off the road, and spent an hour or so taking photographs.

Then I drove on out to the Cannon Ferry Road and headed north. There is a lot more snow out that way, and lots of birds were concentrated along the road shoulders. I saw field sparrows, white-throated sparrows, juncos, cardinals, towhees, brown thrashers, hermit thrushes, mockingbirds, fox sparrows, meadowlarks, mourning doves, phoebes, and killdeers. When I reached the intersection of Cannon Ferry Road and Welch Road the sun started to come out, and I spent several hours along both roads taking photographs.

There were several places where patches of winged sumac grew. The sumacs were full of dried berries, and I was surprised at the many species of birds feeding on them. I photographed robins, white-throated sparrows, hermit thrushes, brown thrashers, mockingbirds, cedar waxwings, and even a phoebe feeding on the dry berries. A mockingbird was trying to defend a patch of sumac bushes along Welch Road and was wearing itself out chasing every bird that came near.

A little farther down Cannon Ferry Road I came upon a turkey vulture walking along the edge of the road. It was holding both wings out, and one wing was broken at the elbow joint. I suspect it had been shot or hit by a car. On seeing me it walked into deep snow in the woods, where it had very heavy going. I could have caught it easily, and was strongly tempted, but catching a vulture can turn out to be a pretty messy affair and I was not exactly dressed for it. Besides, the situation was somewhat like a dog chasing a car—I wasn't exactly sure what I was going to do with it after I caught it!

When I got home I called the Raptor Center in Chapel Hill and found out that they do repair and will try to rehabilitate vultures. They will try to find someone to collect this one or, if no one is available, will ask me to try catch it and take it to Ahoskie or Dr Eddings in Washington for treatment.

9th March 1989

It turned out that the Raptor Center in Charlotte really wanted the turkey vulture that I mentioned last week. It also happened that they couldn't find anyone to come up and capture it, so they talked me into doing it. I cleared it with the Game Protection Officer, and early Monday morning Dorothy and I drove to the area where I had seen it the evening before.

I parked the car, took a blanket, and headed into the swamp, wading through a foot of snow. I found the vulture where I expected it to be, about a hundred yards off the road, sitting about six feet up on the leaning stub of a fallen tree. It let me get quite close, then hopped down and led me on a merry chase through greenbriars, grapevines, and across a wet depression where I got momentarily bogged down knee-deep in sticky peaty mud, before I got close enough to toss a blanket over it. For those of you who have never caught a vulture, be aware that they have the nasty habit of up-chucking their latest meal all over you when you grab them—hence the blanket, to localize the mess and to blind them so they cease to struggle. This one proved to be very nicely behaved, didn't up-chuck, and quieted down when I bundled it up in the blanket. I put it in a cat-traveling case and took it to the Gatesville Medical Center where Dr Jenkins would hold it temporarily until he could find someone to take it to Ahoskie Veterinary Hospital. No one was immediately available, so we decided to take it there ourselves.

The animal hospital in Ahoskie does rehabilitation work on raptors, our birds of prey. They take in injured raptors and do an extensive examination there. If the injuries are not too bad they do the work right there; if the injuries are extensive and severe but the bird responds to treatment, then it is sent by plane to the Raptor Clinic in Charlotte where more complete facilities exist. At either location, when the bird is recovered it is released back into the wild. If it cannot survive back in the wild, through loss of a wing for instance, then it is sent to an educational exhibit where it is kept captive for the rest of its life and used in programs for schools.

We turned the vulture over to Dr Powell at the Veterinary Hospital and watched as it was taken out of the traveling case, had its wing X-rayed, and was finally put into a roomy cage. Throughout it all the vulture was remarkably well-behaved. It just spread its six-foot wings while we held its feet, and didn't struggle. Its upper wingbone had been broken and had started to heal, but the angle was wrong and the vulture would not be able to fly. It will have to be given an injection to put it to sleep while its wingbone is rebroken and pinned at the correct angle. The procedure is complicated, so the vulture will be sent to Grace Smith in Greenville who will put it on a plane for Charlotte, where someone from the Raptor Center will pick it up and take it there for the operation. After rehabilitation it will probably be released back in the area where I found it.

Dr Powell has raised several turkey vultures from hatchlings and says that they make interesting pets. Hers followed her around like little puppies. She took this one to a local school,

TURKEY VULTURE
Cathartes aura

where the children were fascinated by it. It spread its huge wings and walked around accepting tidbits of raw chicken from the braver students. Close-up its not an ugly bird. I called this one "Brutus" because it looked like an ancient dignified Roman with a wrinkled bald head and a big nose, all swaddled up in a black toga.

30th March 1989

A red-shouldered hawk has refurbished her last year's nest and is incubating eggs in the forks of a big white oak near Jay Under-hill's home on the Yeopim River. I'll try to get photographs when the eggs hatch.

4th May 1989

Eggs in a killdeer nest along the road at Drummond Point have hatched, and several tiny long-legged replicas of their parents were following them around when I was out there Monday morning. A killdeer nest in the gravel behind the Rustic Wood Company building on Highway 17 still had four eggs in it on Monday morning. They should hatch any time now.

25th May 1989

The killdeer eggs in the nest behind the Rustic Wood Company building hatched on May 11th. Sally Harrison, who has been watching and worrying over them for three weeks, called at 8 am with the news that two of the eggs had hatched. By the time we arrived, a third egg had hatched. The mother fluttered around, pretending to have a broken wing, and as I crouched by the nest to take photographs she rushed up to my knee, fluffed out all her feathers, and gave me a tremendous scold. When the other egg hatches and the babies dry off, the mother will lead them out into the field where they will forage, much like little quail, with parents guarding and brooding them until they can fly.

15th June 1989

Five young prothonotary warblers at Pettigrew State Park are leading very interesting lives: their parents chose to build their nest behind the grille of the park's new dump truck! No one knew anything about this until last week when the parents were observed leaving the front of the vehicle. Investigation revealed a nest just behind the grille, with five newly hatched chicks in it. According to Sid Shearin, Park Superintendent, the truck has been used almost daily, had been on a thirty-mile run the day the nest was discovered, and had just been washed and waxed! Through it all the mother had somehow managed to incubate the eggs, probably by sitting tight and going along for the rides. The parents now have the job of keeping track of the truck and keeping five babies fed and warm. If they survive to adulthood, they are going to be a bunch of very blasé young warblers.

All four of our children plus two grandchildren were visiting us last week. All of us love the sights and sounds of nature, so every evening at about 8:30 we took a slow drive out Indian Trail Road. There are a lot of fireflies along the roadsides, and we saw lots of deer, including quite a few accompanied by spotted fawns. One evening I turned onto Nixon's Beach Road, drove for about a mile and a half, parked the car, cut off the motor and lights, and we listened to at least three chuck-will's-widows calling from the edge of the woods. These are lovely liquid calls. The bird is like a whip-poor-will but about a third larger, and instead of *whip-poor-will* it says *chuck-will's-widow*. In addition, the ditch along the road is full of narrow-mouthed toads, all calling lustily; they sound like high-pitched, rabbit-sized sheep. Standing there in the warm darkness surrounded by the natural sounds brings back all lost, wild America. It floods over you like a wave—very good for one's soul and one's humility. I highly recommend it!

3rd August 1989

The dump truck at Pettigrew State Park is back in the news! One morning last week I received a phone call from the park superintendent. A barn-owl had somehow become wedged between the dump truck body and the back of the cab. They raised the truck body and the owl dropped down on the chassis where it was sitting, apparently injured. I drove over, fully expecting it to be gone by the time I got there, but it was still there and allowed me to pick it up. It appeared to be an immature bird and had several flight feathers missing from one wing.

I promptly notified the Raptor Center in Charlotte and took the owl to Ahoskie. I was called the next day and informed that nothing was broken. The owl was bruised and still, but it could fly and had eaten a chicken leg overnight. It was therefore decided that the owl's best interests would probably be served by releasing it back in the area where it had been found.

This is a very interesting owl. Its range is worldwide in tropical and temperate regions. It is quite rare in the eastern United States, more common in the west. The barn-owl—alias the "monkey-faced owl," "golden owl," or "knock-kneed owl"—is about sixteen inches tall and has a pure white heart-shaped face. The breast is pale and the back and wings golden with light brown spots. The eyes are dark brown. It has the best hearing of all the owls and in tests will unerringly pounce on mice in a soundproof, totally dark room. It feeds on mice and rats, is highly beneficial, and should never be harmed. While a dozen or so young owls were reported throughout the state this year, I do not think that a single nest was found. To the best of my recollection, this is only the third barn-owl I have ever seen and the first one I have had in my hands.

I took photographs of the owl, showed it to interested people, and that night took it back to Pettigrew State Park and released it. It sat quietly on my fist, turning its head and looking and listening to the night sounds before flying a little awkwardly up into a live oak. The creature appeared to be a little naive and clumsy, but if a horned owl doesn't catch it in the next few nights and it stays away from dump trucks, this barn-owl should live to a ripe old age.

24th August 1989

Probably because of all the wet weather recently, I've been see-ing some of the more unusual waterbirds. A little blue heron was feeding in the pond along the eleventh fairway at the Chowan Country Club, and a flock of fourteen glossy ibis flew low across the same pond. On Sunday afternoon there were about sixty cattle egrets in among the cattle at the C.Y. Parrish farm along High-way 32. The egrets run along behind the cattle and catch grass-hoppers that the cattle flush out of the grass. When the cattle lie down, the egrets will perch on them and catch flies. This doesn't seem to bother the cows; they just chew their cud and ignore the egrets.

7th December 1989

I got an interesting phone call last week from Jay Underhill. He had an albino cormorant sitting on a log in the Yeopim River just in front of his house, so I took the camera and drove over. The cormorant was still there when I arrived. It was a pale ivory in color with a yellow bill. It was sitting on its legs and feet so I could not see what color they were. It appears to be a double-crested cormorant, but I did not have a normal bird nearby for comparison. I took several color photographs and asked Jay to call me when it comes back. I'll take the big Celestron telescope with me and get a much better look.

Sometimes these birds get drowned in the nets of fishermen, so if any local fisherman who reads this happens to find one in their nets, I would appreciate hearing about it. I would like to have a cormorant for the Natural History Museum in Raleigh.

21st December 1989

My sister and her husband spent several days with us last week, and on Thursday I took them to Lake Mattamuskeet to see the wintering waterfowl. The full complement of wintering birds has not arrived yet, but there were several thousand tundra swans, coots, and canvasbacks feeding along the shoreline.

Two adult bald eagles were sitting in the tops of cypress trees on the little island just off the causeway, and a third one was flying over the lake a little farther out. As he swung around and came towards us, the thousands of ducks and coots along his line of flight erupted out of the water with a roar. The eagle was probably hungry and was checking out the flocks to see if there were any injured or sick members that he could catch without a lot of effort.

I spent Friday afternoon at Pettigrew State Park getting things squared away for the Christmas Bird Count. I stayed until dark looking and listening for owls. The sunset over the lake was spectacular, and as the light faded thousands of tundra swans glided low overhead and settled for the night on the lake, their calls making a continuous roar across the water.

18th January 1990

Probably because of the recent heavy freezings, swans are having some problems this year. I counted eighty dead swans along three sections of Lake Phelps shoreline last Sunday. Eagles have been feeding on these dead swans. Matt and I saw one on Sunday afternoon along the south side of the lake: it pitched down from a dead pine and flew low over the lake without giving us too long a look at it. It was either an immature bald eagle or a golden eagle. The overall impression was of a golden eagle, but it will take more observations to tell for sure.

8th February 1990

The Carolina Bird Club held its winter meeting on the Outer Banks last weekend; I spent Saturday there attending several of the bird hikes. I got fairly close to a group of avocets—big shorebirds with long thin upturned bills—and I got several good photographs. There were about seven white pelicans in North Pond on Pea Island; I took several photographs of one swimming around with tundra swans, and several more when it flew overhead.

This is a magnificent bird, the largest in North America, with a wingspread of nine feet or so.

15h March 1990

The pair of red-shouldered hawks who raised a brood in the nest in a big oak at the edge of Jay Underhill's yard have started to build a new nest in another oak about a hundred feet away from the old one. Hawks usually repair the old nests and use them year after year, so I don't know why this pair decided to rebuild. Sometimes an owl, who is an earlier nester, will take over a hawk's nest in early spring and force the hawks to rebuild, but as far as I could see the old nest has simply been abandoned.

19th April 1990

A killdeer constructed a nest in the gravel at the edge of the parking lot at the Country Club and laid three eggs in it. Henry Powell and Dick Taylor discovered it Saturday morning. Dick and I moved part of a broken piece of playground equipment over it to keep cars off it, and I put a sign on it to warn people away. When I finished my round of golf I checked the nest again and found that, in spite of our efforts, some big-footed idiot had somehow managed to get in among the pipes and had stepped on the nest, crushing two of the three eggs. I cleaned up the nest and put the remaining egg in it, and am hoping the female killdeer will re-nest there.

3rd May 1990

Harry and Marginette Lassiter have had an adventure with wood ducks in front of their house. Coming back from a walk they had a hen wood duck explode out of the grass at their feet and flutter along in front of them in a classic "broken wing" act. They saw at once that she had a brood of small ducklings hidden in the grass, so allowed her to lead them along the edge of the road and away from the ducklings. When the mother thought that she had led them far enough away, she took wing and circled across the field, calling the ducklings. In answer to her call they dashed desperately across Route 32.

Marginette tried to stop traffic but the driver of a pick-up truck either did not see her or ignored her and ran through the line of ducklings, killing three of them. The frantic mother gathered the rest of them and led them along a ditch across the field to a flooded area that flows into a swamp on Hayes Plantation. The tiny ducklings were no more than a day old, and there were no trees with nesting holes anywhere near the scene, so I think that the mother duck nested on the ground in the small pines beside the Lassiter house.

17th May 1990

I got an interesting phone call last week from a home owner on the south side of Lake Phelps. When he was straightening up a wood duck box which had been pushed over by ice last winter, a baby owl popped out and fluttered through the water to the edge of the woods. I drove over and found the little owlet perched in a small tree in a flooded section of shoreline. It was a screech-owl, red phase, and about as big as my fist.

When it saw me it drew up real skinny so it looked like an eight-inch section of hoe handle, and pretended to be a dead stub. I picked it up and brought it, bill popping, to show the two young couples at the house. It was pretty well feathered and would have been out of the box in a day or so anyway, so I decided to put it back in thick brush at the edge of the woods. The parents knew where it was and would feed it; in a day or so they would bring the rest of the brood out to join it. One of the parents was nearby, calling to it with a lot of soft whistles and chuckles and threatening me with bill poppings and hissing.

These little owls are flying tigers. As I placed the owlet back in a wax myrtle bush, the parent dived at me, knocked my hat off, and scratched my forehead with all eight claws. I retreated for first aid then went back to get photographs. Just as I was finishing, the parent came in again and hit my wrist with her claws, so I decided to leave her in possession of the field. As we watched, she called the little owlet and it began to scramble along the limb and deeper into the brush. If it grows up as fierce as its mother it will make out just fine!

5th July 1990

I found a nest of a least bittern in thick grass growing in about sixteen inches of water, among the grass stems just above the water-level. There were four white eggs in the nest, and a week later all four had hatched into four of the gawkiest, fuzzy, big-eyed little goblin babies you have ever seen. I put up a blind and spent about four hours photographing the babies and the parents coming in to feed them. The parents are beautiful birds but blend in so well with the grass stems, through which they slip like shadows, that I never saw them until they appeared like magic at the edge of the nest to disgorge frogs and minnows for the hungry nestlings.

The least bittern, while a common breeder in our marshes, is rarely seen. It lives deep in the marsh grass and cattails, and rarely flies. It is our smallest heron, about the size of a mourning dove. It is very secretive. In a lifetime of observing birds I have seen fewer than two dozen of them.

19th July 1990

One of the farm roads that leads to one of my bat colonies goes through a swamp and has several big culverts going under it. During the recent dry weather the stream in the swamp has dried up except for a pool at each end of the culvert. All kinds of wildlife are concentrated at these pools, and it is an ideal place to get pictures. The deepest pool is about six feet wide and thirty feet long and was so overgrown with trees, bushes, and vines, and was so dark, that one almost needed a flashlight in order to see anything.

I spent several hours there last week with clippers, saw, and machete, letting in a lot of light while keeping the area natural.

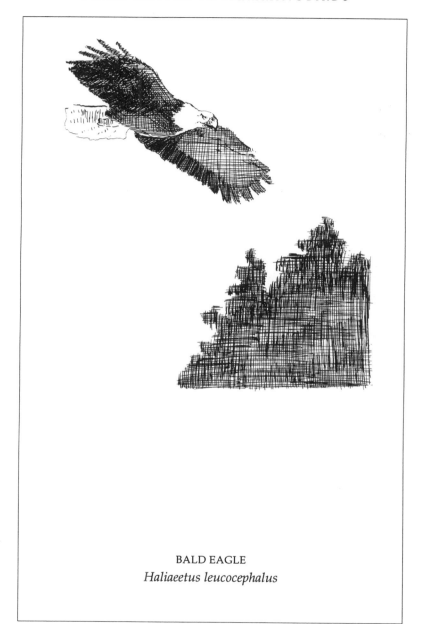

BALD EAGLE
Haliaeetus leucocephalus

I can sit in the car with the big telephoto resting on the window and get photographs of the various creatures as they come to drink, bathe, or feed. Being in the car keeps me away from yellowflies, ticks, and chiggers, but it gets almighty hot, and after several hours I'm almost melted down!

A lot of bird species are around the pool. A pair of green-backed herons slip in and out, hunting minnows; a shy, secretive Louisiana waterthrush teeters around catching insects at the water's edge; and prothonotary warblers come in to take a bath in the shallow water.

2nd August 1990

I've logged about fifteen hours of quiet observing at my small pool in the woods. Half a dozen small species of birds slip in to take a bath in the shallow water, and a little green-backed heron slips like a ghost in and out of the shadows as it hunts minnows and crayfish.

27th December 1990

On my way home from a day at Pungo Lake last Friday I saw what I thought was a road-killed hawk alongside the road. I backed up and found an alive but dazed juvenile red-tailed hawk glaring at me. I threw a jacket over it, carefully avoiding its dangerous talons. The hawk was still alive the next morning, so I drove with it to the Ahoskie Veterinary Hospital. It proved to have a concussion but no broken bones. It was a young-of-the-year bird, in good shape, and a prime candidate for release back to the wild when it stops seeing stars and the world stays right side up.

10h January 1991

Two pairs of bald eagles are new residents of Chowan County, one pair at each end. I have been watching an adult eagle at this end of the county for several years but it has always been a loner. This year, however, it took up with a teenager, a juvenile bird which has not acquired the white head and tail of the mature bird. The pair is staying together and have constructed a nest.

I talked to Tom Henson, State Eagle Coordinator, about this pair, and he says that quite often a new pair consists of an adult and a juvenile and that they usually "play house" the first year and don't attempt to raise a family until the second year. This makes sense for them. They mate for life and stay in their territory year round. They require a large home territory with an adequate food supply and, above all, a large core nesting area where they are not disturbed by people.

Eagles are large birds, with wing spans of about eight feet. This means that each wing, spread out, is about the size of an ironing board. There is no way that a mature bald eagle can be mistaken for anything else, and the $20,000 fine for shooting one should keep them safe. The juvenile, however, are dark brown and won't get their white heads and tails until they are four years old. I am concerned that someone will shoot at the juvenile eagle of this pair.

Tom said that another pair had taken up residence at the northern end of the county, and that Chowan County is the only county with two nesting pairs. The bald eagle is recovering from a near brush with extinction. I think that it has been around half a century since a pair nested here, so observe them and enjoy them.

14th February 1991

I'm becoming a bit involved with owls this month.

On February 2nd I led a bird walk at Pettigrew State Park for about ten people. Along the Carriage Trail I found a screech-owl sitting in a hollow in a big beech limb. It was close to the group and we all got a very gook look at it. screech-owls come in two color phases and this one was the red phase. In the north the red phase is rather rare but in the south the red phase and the gray phase are split about fifty-fifty. All-gray parents can have both red and gray offspring in the same brood. I wasn't carrying my big telephoto lens at the time but came back later and, by kissing the back of my hand and making squeaking noises, I lured the little owl back into the entrance hole and took several photos. I have checked it several times this week, and on warm sunny days have found it at the entrance from about 2 to 3 PM. I'll keep an eye on it this spring in case it's a nest hollow, in which case I may get photos of fuzzy owlets. Incidentally, we saw twenty-eight other bird species on the two-hour walk.

Last Tuesday Jim Merritt and I were at the Chowan Golf Course checking trees that might have to be removed. We had just decided that a big hollow stub with a big side branch would have to come down when I walked around it and discovered a lot of soft owl-down feathers caught in vines around a hollow about fifteen feet up. I knew at once that there was an owl nest there but wasn't sure if it was a barred or a great horned owl. Jim had a ladder, but I wasn't about to poke my nose into a great horned owl's nest! I came back just before dark and saw a great horned owl enter the hollow. I have been observing the nest from the Number 4 tee through a 40x Celestron telescope. The big female sits on the nest and stares back. If the eggs haven't hatched already, they will very soon. We will not cut this tree, and I expect to get a series of photos of the owls rearing their brood.

This is the largest and fiercest North-American owl, and the parents can be unpredictable around the nest. In the past I have banded young horned owls in the nest and usually the parents just fuss from a nearby tree, but on one occasion the big female came in and ripped a long gash in the back of a padded jacket I was wearing. We have put stakes around the nest tree and asked golfers to take a free drop outside the staked area if they hit a ball near the tree; discretion is the better part of valor.

Like all our owls, the great horned owl is highly beneficial, eating a lot of rats. It is big enough to take squirrels, possums, muskrats, half-grown cats, and in the north-eastern states is one of the few predators that will catch and eat skunks. On the debit side, if you raise ducks and chickens who range outside, then great-horned owls are *not* good neighbors. This pair have been catching some ring-billed gulls on the golf course but, looking at their pellets, I find that they are mostly eating rats.

28th March 1991

The great horned owl nest has been abandoned. When the female stayed off the nest for three days I climbed up and looked in. There was only one egg and it was quite cold. Something must have happened to the female: maybe it was hit by a car or some other injury.

I have found three other horned owl nests this year: one near Cherry, one at Pungo Lake, and one at a campground in Manteo. The one in Manteo has two very large owlets crowding the nest. The one at Pungo is in a last-year's crow's nest and I don't think the eggs have hatched yet. The one at Cherry is in a hollow tree and I can't tell if there are young in the nest or not.

20th June 1991

I have another little observation pool in the woods in back of our house where a stream crosses under a farm road. With the dry weather the stream is drying up, and the deep pool at the culvert is a magnet for all kinds of wildlife. I use the car as a blind and I am back there for several hours almost every day, photographing and observing the wildlife that shows up. I am in the slow and delicate process of cutting and trimming brush around the pool to let in more light for photography without destroying its attraction for wildlife.

A dozen or so species of birds regularly come to bathe in the shallow water at the back edge of the pool. This is the one spot where I can go and see waterthrushes. These small warblers are essentially ground dwellers and walk, not hop, in the shadows around the pool, their bodies bobbing up and down like yo-yos.

Last Sunday I saw something interesting. A cottonmouth was swimming slowly down the length of the pool when a large flock of grackles was passing through. The grackles appeared fascinated by the snake. Twenty or so surrounded it, walking along the shore keeping pace with it and hopping in the brush overhead. They kept out of reach but did not appear to be alarmed, and only left when the snake crawled out of the water and coiled up under a bush.

4th July 1991

Last week I got a phone call from Gail Kelly at Girls Incorporated of the Albemarle in Elizabeth City. They have a nighthawk nesting on the graveled roof just outside a window on the second floor. We drove over, and the nighthawk allowed me to raise the window and take several photographs from a distance of about fourteen feet. Gail said that this same bird nested there last year and raised one nestling. I'll try to go over at least once a week and get a series of color slides of the rearing process.

Nighthawks are semi-precocial, which means that the nestling will not stay in the little hollow his mother has scooped out but will wander about in the gravel on the roof until it is able to fly, in about twenty-one days, so I should be able to get a series of photographs of its development. These birds fly at dusk and dawn. If I'm lucky I may get photographs of the parent feeding the nestling.

18th July 1991

From now until the end of August we will have large flocks of purple martins and other native swallows passing through the area on their way to their wintering ground in South America. Their favorite roosting and staging area is the Chowan River Bridge. This is also the spot where thousands are killed each year by traffic. They gather at dusk to roost on and under the bridge, become confused by car headlights, and are killed by the fast-moving traffic. David Lee, Curator of Birds at the NC Museum of Natural Sciences in Raleigh, says that the Chowan River Bridge is notorious for the number of swallows killed there.

Dr Francis, who travels across this bridge daily, estimates that the total martin kill at this bridge throughout the season equals or exceeds the number of young birds that are reared in this area each year. He has written to the North Carolina Wildlife Resources Commission about the problem, and I have called several bird people around the state. As soon as we find the right agency to contact, I will start putting a little pressure on the appropriate people to get the problem solved. In the mean time, what we can do is drive slowly and carefully across the bridge in the evening when the birds are flying.

16th January 1992

Friday and Saturday, January 10th and 11th, were the target dates for the 1992 Midwinter Bald Eagle Survey. The survey is used to assess eagle populations, identify over-wintering areas, and to locate possible breeding pairs. We have been keeping an eye on the pair out along the Yeopim River who showed up in 1990 and constructed a nest in the top of a tall pine about a quarter of a mile inland from the river. This is the pair consisting of a mature eagle with white head and tail and an immature eagle who was all brown. They simply "played house" last year while they staked out a territory. The mature one has been observed almost weekly for the last three months, and two mature ones were seen by Fred Inglis last Friday. We hope that this pair will not be disturbed by logging operations and will nest this year, joining the pair that is nesting along the upper Chowan River.

30th January 1992

A flock of about half a dozen brown pelicans moved into the area about a month ago. They have been observed from Edenton Bay to Drummond Point. Last Sunday I spent an hour with the camera set up on the beach at Drummond Point, photographing three pelicans as they dove for fish.

On Drummond Point, about a hundred yards from the end of the road by the old collapsed barn, there are several large privet bushes full of fruit. These are not native species and are often quite invasive, but they are an important source of food for wintering birds. I parked the car at the side of the road there and photographed brown thrashers, white-throated sparrows, yellow-rumped warblers, cardinals, song sparrows, a mockingbird, and a hermit thrush eating the blue fruit of the privet. The sparrows and cardinals were discarding the pulp and eating the seeds, their blue beaks stained deep blue by the berry juice; the other species simply swallowed the entire fruit.

While I was there a sharp-shinned hawk attempted to catch one of the white-throated sparrows and created havoc among the feeding birds. The sparrows and juncos took refuge under the collapsed barn; the other species simply froze where they sat, not moving or blinking an eye until the sharpshin left.

13th February 1992

We went out to Fred and Jeannie Inglis's at Somerset Farm to see if any of our study colony of big-eared bats were in the barn. They were not, but while we were standing around talking to Fred a male Wilson's warbler began to forage in the boxwood beside us. This is a small, bright yellow bird, and the male has a black skullcap. It's an uncommon warbler and should be in South America at this time of the year. I photographed it and called the Rare Bird Alert in Raleigh to report its presence. It will probably be a January record for North Carolina.

I got a call Friday from Dr Bob Gaines at the NC Veterinary Diagnostic Lab: a small owl had gotten into a lab room. I went over and we captured it. It was a grey-phase screech-owl, probably a male, the smallest screech-owl I have ever handled. We admired its beautiful plumage then released it. It popped its beak at us a few times before flying back into the pine woods.

FROM HAWKS TO HUMMINGBIRDS

27th February 1992

The little Wilson's warbler who has been hanging around the barn at Somerset has disappeared, but last Friday I saw two other birds who were rushing the season. A yellow-breasted chat and a female orchard oriole showed up at Fort Landing on the Alligator River—the chat on the road leading to the landing, and the oriole at Willy and Feather Phillips's bird feeder at the landing. ospreys are arriving and inspecting their old nests, getting ready for a new season. All in all, folks, spring it is a-coming.

26th March 1992

A pair of brown-headed nuthatches are excavating a nest hole in a pine stub beside the Number 7 tee at the Country Club. These are feisty, energetic little birds of open pine woodland and, like all members of the nuthatch species, don't seem to care whether they are rightside up or upside down!

7th July 1992

I spent last Friday afternoon at Pettigrew State Park getting a series of photographs of a newly discovered hummingbird's nest on a low pine branch. In the eight years that we have lived here, I have found fourteen hummingbird nests in the woods around our house, but all of them have been high up, and all in beech trees. I hope this one at the park is successful in hatching and rearing her twins as the location is ideal for photography.

As I sat on a bench in the main picnic area at the park I was startled by a series of whoops and bloodcurdling screams from the nearby woods as a pair of barred owls started up a dialogue. In a few minutes one of them flew into the tree over my head and sat in the entrance hole of a big hollow about sixty feet above the ground. It was the female and she sat there hooting softly for about ten minutes, allowing me to take a series of photographs before she flew off silently into the woods. I'm pretty sure that the pair have a nest in the hollow, and I'll keep tabs on it, hoping to get photographs of the parents carrying food items for the young. I've always been curious about the nature of barred owls' prey, and this will be an opportunity to make some observations.

22nd October 1992

The advance guard of our wintering kestrels has arrived, and their family groups are becoming a common sight on power lines along our roads.

5th November 1992

Last week I saw two huge Caspian terns over Lake Phelps and photographed an American redstart, one of our more uncommon wood warblers, in a flock of our most common winter warbler, the yellow-rumped. A few tundra swans have showed up on Lake Mattamuskeet, and about a thousand were on North Pond at Pea Island when we were there last Thursday.

3rd December 1992

As a warm-up for the Christmas Counts, I spent Sunday at Lake Mattamuskeet, birding along the causeway and the entrance road. There are lots of tundra swans and coots but not too many ducks and geese as yet. Among the swans along the causeway was one coal-black swan. It was the same size as the snow white tundra swans and really stood out. Black swans are native to Australia; this one probably escaped from a zoo or private collection.

A pair of bald eagles flew over the north end of the causeway, creating consternation among vast flocks of coots as they flew overhead. One of the eagles was a mature bird with white head and tail, the other was an immature. They went through a series of aerial maneuvers, looping around each other in what I think were courtship rituals. The smaller eagle, the immature male, was the aggressor, diving at the larger female repeatedly.

17th December 1992

There is a red-shouldered hawk who perches on the power-line along our driveway and doesn't seem to be bothered by the car as we come and go. Last Thursday I stopped the car about fifty yards from it and observed it through the binoculars. As I watched, it suddenly dived into the grass and seized something in its talons. After considerable flapping and tugging, it pulled a large hispid rat into the driveway and flew into the woods with it. When it pulled the rat out, the reason for all the struggles became clear. In seizing the rat it also seized grass stems. It wouldn't release its death grip on the rat, so had to rip out the grass by the roots as well!

Another incident with a raptor was frustrating as well as interesting. I discovered an unusual, large, sparrow-like bird in the grass at the edge of a flooded area. I took several photographs of it at close range but could not identify it, so I put the camera down and began to leaf through several bird books to try to find out what it was. I heard a sharp call, and looked up to find a kestrel gripping and mantling the bird. I reached for the camera, turned back to the bird, only to find that the kestrel had flown off with it. Kestrels usually don't fly very far, but despite looking for half an hour or so I could find no trace of it. I still don't know what the strange bird was, but when I get the photos back I'll send one to the rare bird center in Raleigh to get it identified.*

Several good birders from Greenville and the Raleigh area have reported seeing short-eared owls on the Tyson Farms just south of Lake Phelps, and I am spending some time over there trying to locate them. I haven't found them as yet, but I have found something else very interesting.

On Tuesday of last week I jumped an immature bald eagle from behind a screen of weeds along an irrigation ditch running through a field that was full of tundra swans. As I got closer, I saw that the eagle had been feeding on the carcass of a swan. I examined the carcass closely. The white feathers were quite bloody and its joints were still flexible. From these I think that

* It proved to be a female bobolink.

the eagle made the kill himself instead of scavenging an already dead bird. Eagles will not bother swans in the water because, while they are capable of killing swans, they could not lift them from the water. I have not heard of bald eagles killing swans before, but theoretically they should have no problem on land. Yesterday I found another swan carcass in the same field, killed and fed on just like the first one, so apparently one eagle at least is learning how to do it.

4th February 1993

The bald eagle is making a come-back in North Carolina. The 1992 mid-winter eagle survey registered sixty-nine eagles sighted in the state, the highest total since the survey was begun in 1983. Known breeding territories now total nine for the state, with five active nests during the 1992 season. In four of the territories nests were built, but no active nesting has yet occurred. Aerial monitoring of the five active nests showed a production of seven eaglets in 1992.

The active nest up the Chowan River produced one eaglet last year. The pair of eagles whose territory extends from Drummond Point on Albemarle Sound to Bethel at the upper end of the Yeopim River have built two nests but have not activated either one as yet. I have been observing this pair for two years, and Fred Inglis and Jay Underhill and other residents notify me of any sightings along the Yeopim. The pair in this territory consists of a mature eagle with white head and tail and an immature all-brown bird. This pair has been playing house for the last two years and may now be ready to get down to business.

There are two osprey nests in dead cypress trees on Drummond Point, and I always check these when I'm out that way. Last Sunday the immature eagle was sitting in one of the osprey nests and the adult was perched on a limb close by. I was able to get several photos through the big telephoto lens and observe them for ten minutes before they took off and flew up the Yeopim River.

Bald eagles will sometimes take over an osprey's nest as their own, so I will keep a sharp eye on this one as well as checking out the nest the eagles built in a tall pine back from the water last year.

18th February 1993

By Valentine's Day signs of spring are already showing up in the Coastal Plains of the Carolinas. It may not look like spring, and it may not feel like spring—we may even get a little snow squall or two before spring is fully upon us—but in the woods and swamps signs are there if we look and listen.

Woodcocks are making their courting fights. I heard one Monday at dusk in the field between the headquarters at Pettigrew State Park and Somerset Place. The male takes off and ascends in wide circles, uttering a loud, nasal *peent* as he climbs almost out of sight. Then he power-dives to earth in wild zig-zags, still calling loudly, with the wind whistling shrilly through his stiffened wing feathers.

Jay Underhill called me Sunday night. He had found a dead golden-crowned kinglet on the lawn in his backyard. I collect road- and lawn-kills of birds and animals in good condition for the State Museum, so I went out and picked it up. Golden-crowned kinglets are small birds, not quite as big as a chickadee, with a broad golden stripe across the top of their heads. Their summer habitat is coniferous forests, preferably spruces. Their nests are built of mosses, lichens, fine strips of inner bark, and quite often lined with grouse feathers with quills pointing downward, tips arching over the eggs. The nest is built out near the ends of horizontal spruce limbs, blends in with spruce foliage, and is very difficult to see from the ground. I have found only one nest, and only found it by observing a parent bird carrying food to nestlings.

4th March 1993

A few hardy birds are starting to filter through on their way north. We have a few killdeers here all winter, but I am beginning to see a lot more of them in the wet fields these last few days; they are starting to call more frequently as well.

A lot of hermit thrushes are showing up as well. I counted eighteen along Indian Trail Road and the road out to Drummond Point. The road surface absorbs the heat from the sun then radiates it into the soil of each side of the road and the air above it, creating a micro climate around it. Hardy flying insects are attracted to the road surface, and insects in the warmed soil of the road shoulders are activated. This is attracting both hermit thrushes and a lot of robins. The thrushes are also feeding on berries of the sumac trees and the smilax vine. Fortunately, these berries are not the first choice of our wintering birds and are usually left for last, forming a source of emergency rations for very early migrants. The most favored berries are dogwood, holly, and, surprisingly, poison ivy.

Large flocks of cedar waxwings are passing through the Edenton area right now; last Saturday several thousand were feeding on berries of holly and red cedar in the ellipse in front of Hayes Plantation. I parked my car there to watch them—and got thoroughly covered with purple bird droppings for my pains! During all the commotion a little sharp-shinned hawk slipped in and took one of the waxwings, whereupon they all took off with a roar, streaming by me close enough to ruffle my hair.

1st April 1993

Brown pelicans are becoming more common around the Edenton waterfront this month. I spend some time each week sidewalk-superintending the construction of the Hayes Plantation bridge, and one has been keeping me company, sitting either on the railing at the corner of the park or on a piling just offshore. Several have been spending the winter near Drummond Point and up and down the Yeopim River. Brown pelicans are well back from their brush with extinction some years ago due to eggshell thinning from pesticide contamination, and are apparently expanding their breeding range northward. We can expect that they will become more common around the Albemarle region as time passes.

15th April 1993

I got a call from a graduate student at Duke University who is studying the plight of our songbirds who nest in deciduous woods. She monitors them on their wintering ground in Costa Rica and is setting up a study area along the Roanoke River to monitor their breeding success here. She is especially concerned with the wood thrush and will be mist-netting and banding birds here as well as in Costa Rica. She will be needing help, so I have volunteered to help out.

29th April 1993

A lot of our spring birds are back. I led a Nature Conservancy tour into a white cedar swamp along the Scuppernong River last week, and we saw prothonotary, parula, and yellow-throated warblers. These are all birds that nest in swamp forest habitats.

A pair of house finches are nesting in the ivy around a light-post out on Country Club Drive, and another pair are nesting somewhere close to the clubhouse entrance at the Country Club.

3rd June 1993

I observed a wildly improbably situation in Manteo last week. The DeMents, who live in Burnside Woods, have an osprey nest on a platform close to their deck, and something very unusual was going on: an escaped parakeet was sharing the nest! It showed up several weeks ago, and at first the ospreys tried to drive it away; but it persisted and after several days the female osprey apparently adopted it. Diane DeMent has seen the female feeding it fish on several occasions, and it is helping to rebuild the nest after a storm partially demolished it. I stopped by their house last Friday. The little parakeet was busily carrying sticks up to the nest for the female to arrange to her satisfaction. I took a series of photographs, and left the little parakeet hard at work ferrying up sticks.

17th June 1993

This time of year every year I'm swamped with requests to raise human-imposed orphans, mostly birds. Well-meaning people see a young bird on the ground and jump to the conclusion that it has been abandoned; they pick it up, take it home, and attempt to rear it. Lots of problems arise.

Most people attempt to feed the young bird bread soaked in milk, not a proper diet for birds. Most birds are insectivores, and the young require incredible amounts of soft-bodied insects. The parents feed them about every ten minutes during daylight hours and remove the droppings to keep the nest clean. Human foster parents are nowhere near that devoted. What happens is that they become overwhelmed by all the attention a young bird needs and the mess it makes, and they look around for help. A good percentage of them get referred to me. I am not a wildlife rehabilitator; that is a full-time job and you have to have a state license to do it. Birds are protected by both state and federal laws, and when anyone takes home a baby bird they are technically breaking both state and federal laws.

So, what do you do if you are tender-hearted and come upon a young bird on the ground? First of all: leave it alone. It has devoted parents who know perfectly well where it is and are off rustling food for it. If it's in the street you can move it to a lawn or brush by the road; it's an old wives' tale that by touching it you will alienate its parents from it. If it's in your yard and you have a cat, keep the cat inside for several days. Birds grow very fast and within two days of leaving the nest they can fly well and have become quite wary.

Occasionally you may find a very small featherless nestling on the ground. It has almost always fallen from a nearby nest. Finding the nest and replacing the nestling is the best solution in this case. It is almost impossible to rear such a young bird.

29th July 1993

I got a call last week from someone in Cape Colony who said she had a bluebird problem. She has a nesting pair in the backyard who are raising nestlings in a box about ten feet from the back of her house. The male has become super macho and is fighting his reflection in all the windows of her house; in the process he's making a mess of the screens on the lower half of the windows.

He thinks that the reflection is a rival, and he's simply trying to drive the rival away. This is a common occurrence with mockingbirds and cardinals, who are routinely sighted fighting their reflections in the hubcaps of cars and in car sideview mirrors, but it is not so common in bluebirds.

This male has a favorite window that is really plastered, but has not neglected the rest of the windows either—they are all dirtied with droppings. I suggested that she tape a strip of red or yellow crepe paper across each window where the bird sits to fight his reflection; this might keep him away. As soon as the pair fledge their brood they will leave, and maybe this male won't be back to raise his third brood in her yard. Meanwhile, this bluebird is wearing out his welcome fast!

30th September 1993

Kermit Layton bands a few mallards each year. Last week he received a letter from the coast of southern Alaska: one of his banded mallards was found dead there on a Pacific Ocean beach. From its number Kermit knew it was one he had banded four years ago. This was a duck who liked to travel! A northwest flyway from here doesn't exist, so we'll never know how or why this mallard ended up so far from home.

18th November 1993

Owls are becoming increasingly active in the woods as winter advances. The big horned owl is the most vocal as well as the largest. The big female in particular is the terror of the woods at night for most of our small mammals. Where skunks are common they are preyed on extensively by horned owls; I have banded young horned owls who smelled strongly of skunk musk. They will take half-grown cats, and a hungry owl will even take on a full-grown one. They are one of the few predators who relish adult seagulls, and when they locate a roosting flock on a dock at night they will come night after night and kill and eat a gull right in the midst of the roosting flock. One such owl has discovered roosting flocks of laughing gulls on the boat docks at Pettigrew State Park and has taken one gull a night for several nights last week.

2nd December 1993

I took advantage of our fine weather of the past week to lead a nature walk through the woods at Pettigrew State Park. We did not see very many land birds, but with thirty people wading through the leaves and talking I didn't really expect to see many. Lake Phelps is beginning to acquire its winter population of water birds. There are laughing gulls, ring-billed gulls, Forster's terns, and even a pair of Caspian terns, our largest tern, as big as a herring gull. Several hundred tundra swans plus a sizable number of Canada geese were also rafting far out in the lake. Closer to shore we jumped flocks of hooded mergansers, wood ducks, black ducks, mallards, and even a pair of early migrating common loons.

16th December 1993

I've been doing quite a bit of traveling between Edenton and Ahoskie during the past two weeks.

Two weeks ago someone found a barred owl sitting dazed by the side of the road. This kind Samaritan threw a towel over the owl, put it in a cardboard box, and took it to our local vet. The vet called me and I picked it up and took it to the Animal Hospital in Ahoskie. They determined that it had a concussion and a broken wing, would probably respond well to therapy, and could be released back into the wild.

Then last Thursday I got another call from our vet—another owl had been turned in. This one was a real jewel, a rare barn-owl, a species that the State of North Carolina is especially concerned about. This one had been picked up in Creswell. Upon examination it proved to have a broken wing, and an X-ray of the wing showed that it had been shot. One number-six shotgun pellet was still lodged near the break. I might point out that it is against the law to shoot any raptor, and substantial fines are levied if the perpetrators are caught. The barn-owl is totally beneficial. It feeds exclusively on mice and rats, and a hungry family might polish off three dozen a night. This one was a young bird, and if antibiotics could cure the extensive infection it would have a good chance to recover and be released.

A third raptor, a male kestrel, was picked up beside the road near New Hope, apparently hit by a car, the extent of its injuries unknown. Unlike the owls, this little bird, our smallest falcon, does not nest here and is a winter migrant only.

This is the best time of the year to observe raptors. The big redtails, our year-round hawks, show up easily against the leafless trees, and the migrant Cooper's and sharpshins soon find that our feeders attract flocks of small birds, and they come hunting through our yards several times a day. I'm not too happy about this, but I like raptors and console myself with the thought that they only catch the sick, injured, or stupid ones and thus keep the survivors healthy and smart.

... I'm just back from the vet's in Ahoskie. The little kestrel has an injured wing and skinned knees but is bright and alert and will be released when its wing is healed. The barred owl has been sent to the Rehab Center in Greenville. Its wing is healing, but it has a detached retina so it cannot be released into the wild. It has been requested by a director of school programs, and when the wing is healed it will be sent to her. Birds in these programs become quite tame and are very useful in educating students about aspects of our natural heritage. The barn-owl is releasable. It will be sent to Greenville for rehabilitation and eventually released back in the area where it was found. While I was there, its loud moans, shrieks, and hisses let everyone know that it wants out—now!

3th February 1994

Birding friends from New York State spent several days with us last week and we went to Mattamuskeet on Saturday. The lake was pretty well frozen over, the ice about two inches thick, so there were not too many waterfowl on the lake itself. The impoundments along the headquarters drive were more open, and a lot of waterfowl were visible here. coots were all over the road, feeding in the grass. On dry land they are not the least duck-like, running about rapidly like chickens.

Several hunched-over, disgruntled great blue herons and great egrets were also stalking through the grass. It was much too cold for frogs, so I presume that they were hunting mice; the great blues, at least, are known to do this and will take unwary small birds as well.

A flock of shovelers was feeding in an area of thin ice. I took photographs of their struggles as a line of four abreast marched across thin ice—taking a few steps, breaking through, struggling up on the ice again, waddling a foot or so then breaking through again—their progress marked by a series of holes across the ice. Their solemn demeanor, coupled with their huge beaks and brilliant colors, made them look like clowns taking prat falls.

17th February 1994

The bad weather of the last two weeks has kept me more or less housebound, but I did put on boots one day last week and went sloshing through the woods. Surprisingly, in spite of our unusual cold spell, things were about on schedule.

I flushed a woodcock from underfoot and very slowly and

quietly followed it for half an hour or so, managing to get one good close-up photograph as it crouched among the leaves. It was so well camouflaged that when I would take my eyes off it I would have to make an effort to find it again. They are probably doing their courtship flights and songs already, and a good place to witness and hear them is in the fields around the canoe-launching area at Merchants Millpond State Park just about dusk.

Crows have been harassing horned owls back in the woods behind Jubilee Farm every day for the past several weeks, and I think that the owls are nesting there. I'll go over there in a week or so and check it out.

There is a small flock of ring-necked ducks on the pond at Village Creek. We only see these ducks around here during the late winter and very early spring as they stop over briefly on their way north to their breeding ground in small ponds in the north central United Sates, Canada, and Alaska. I have been trying to get some close-up photographs of this striking duck, but these ones are quite wary.

3rd March 1994

I spent Sunday at Lake Mattamuskeet trying to locate a spot along the wildlife drive where I can photograph some of our marsh birds. I did find a spot where I saw a lone Virginia rail, but it vanished before I could even get the camera on it. Sitting quietly in the car, I was approached quite closely by a house wren, an orange-crowned warbler, and both ruby-crowned and golden-crowned kinglets. I exposed a full role of film on these little perpetual-motion birds, and I hope I will have one or two good shots of each.

Most of the waterfowl have left for their breeding ground. I didn't see any swans on the lake, and only a dozen geese. Several ospreys are back; one caught a quite large fish and proceeded to eat it in a tree across the marsh from where I had my blind.

ADVENTURES WITH BIRDS

17th March 1994

We have a pair of bald eagles nesting in Chowan County! The pair that I have been observing out on Drummond Point and along the Yeopim River for the past three years have finally decided to set up housekeeping. They built a new nest this winter, and when I checked it out with my 45x Celestron telescope last Thursday I could see the head of a mature eagle as she sat on the nest looking around. This pair have built several nests before but have been, in general, just playing house. Since the female has been observed on this nest for several days, I think that they mean business this time.

I have notified all the State agencies involved with eagles and other endangered species and they will institute a very discreet monitoring of the nest to make sure that the eagles are not disturbed. There is a horrendous fine for harming an eaglet—I think that it starts at $25,000 dollars—and while no one in their right mind would shoot one, well-meaning but curious observers near the nest could cause it to be abandoned. The nest will be monitored from a light plane during the next two weeks to see if eggs have been laid.

Our local Canada geese are beginning to nest. A pair out near Greenfield have pre-empted an osprey nest in a cypress tree just offshore and, unless the ospreys return and oust them, they will nest there. When the young hatch they will just jump out of the nest into the water below. Actually, it's a very safe, secure place for geese to nest, albeit an unusual one. Foxes and other ground predators can't bother them, and raccoons are not apt to swim out and climb the tree.

Unofficially, I guess that spring has arrived in Edenton: the cedar waxwings are here! Starting last week I have observed a dozen or so flocks, altogether about a thousand birds, orbiting over downtown Edenton. They are migrating birds on their way north and have stopped off here as they do every year to eat the

CEDAR WAXWING
Bombycilla cedrorum

heavy crop of holly and cedar berries and the fruits of Bradford pears and hawthorns.

They will hang around for several weeks until most of the berries are gone, and then abruptly one morning they will all be gone. While they are here, though, don't park your car or hang wash under any tree they perch in, for if you do it will be liberally blotched with purple droppings.

Flocks of these birds will sit quietly in tall leafless trees, then at some signal all will descend on a holly tree and feed in a seething mass of fluttering wings for five minutes or so, then abruptly all will leave to perch quietly in the top of a tree while they digest the berries.

14th April 1994

Last weekend I spent a pleasant two days at Lake Mattamuskeet. warbler migrants were moving through; I saw black-and-white warblers, pine warblers, yellow-throated warblers, parulas, blue-gray gnatcatchers, and white-eyed vireos. Most of the waterfowl have left the lake and impoundments, but lots of egrets and herons are taking their place.

I am keeping up a light monitoring of the nesting eagles. They are feeding at least one eaglet. I can see its little down-covered head sticking up as the adults feed it tidbits of fish. This nest is one of only eight nests in the entire state, and we have hopes that it will become a productive one, producing one or two young eagles each year.

5th May 1994

The little eaglet is growing like a weed and is now about as large as a ted-tailed hawk. It is feeding itself, energetically tearing off mouthfuls of flesh from whatever the two adults bring to the nest. They mostly bring in fish, but once I saw them bring in a muskrat or half-grown nutria. The eaglet now has a wingspan of about four feet but no wing feathers yet, so it sits on the edge of the nest flapping its skinny wings as it exercises its wing muscles.

I believe that this pair of adults had another, undiscovered, nest last year and raised a pair of young from it. A pair of immature eagles were following them around during the winter, and last week as I watched the nest, one of the immatures attempted to follow the female back to the nest as she returned from a fishing trip. When they got close to the nest the big female turned on the immature, and the two put on a spectacular aerial show as the more experienced adult rounded up the immature and sent it packing.

These two immatures may hang around the area for a year or so but will eventually wander up and down the coast for three or four years while they mature and get their white heads and tails. As mature eagles they may very well come back to this area to stake out a territory, nest, and raise young. This is prime bald eagle habitat.

26th May 1994

Last week Gus Koch and I were walking through his wooded property in back of his sawmill just off Route 17 between here and Hertford; he has a beautiful and interesting mature mixed hardwood forest. While walking through a bed of ferns we flushed an ovenbird from underfoot. Without moving our feet we parted the ferns carefully and discovered her nest, a neat little roofed-over structure in the fallen leaves with three eggs inside.

9th June 1994

On a warm Sunday several weeks ago a group of us launched canoes on the Bennett Millpond area of the Albemarle Recreation and Leadership Training Center for Disabled Persons. The center wants to develop the Bennett Millpond as a recreation area for both disabled persons and the community at large. Aquatic sports, hiking, and nature trails will be featured. The purpose of this canoe trip was to get a firsthand look at the flora and fauna of the millpond itself. It is a wild and beautiful area.

On the way up the millpond we passed close to an anhinga.

This was an unusual sighting for this large waterbird, whose common names include water turkey and snakebird, and if it nests here it is a first for the Coastal Plains this far north. It took off and soared high over the millpond.

We canoed past several very large beaver lodges, and saw several flocks of Canada geese and ducks of several species. A pair of ospreys were busy constructing a nest in one of the cypress trees out in the millpond, the first that I am aware of in a millpond in this area. We put up several turkey vultures along the forested high ground; they may nest here as well.

I spent some time Saturday at Pettigrew State Park helping out with one of their fishing clinics for children. While there I discovered an indigo bunting nest in a wild rose bush down in a ditch; both adults were feeding nestlings. That same afternoon I discovered the nest of a pair of red-headed woodpeckers. The nest was about one hundred feet up in a huge dead tulip poplar along the Carriage Trail. Both adults were feeding nestlings as I watched. This woodpecker is not common in the Coastal Plain, and I was glad to see a successful nesting. Its low numbers and lack of breeding success is due mainly to competition from the imported starling. When a woodpecker completes a nest hole it is attacked and harassed by several pairs of starlings and is eventually driven away or killed by them; as a consequence its numbers are falling.

The young eaglet is about the size of the adult now but with shorter wing feathers. It spends a lot of time sitting on the edge of the nest, preening and flapping its wings. I suspect it will take its first flight sometime during the next two weeks.

23rd June 1994

At my last look, Saturday morning, the young eaglet was still in the nest. An adult brought in a fish while I watched, and began to nip off strips of flesh and pass them over to the hungry eaglet. The adult left after a few moments, and the young eagle then began to feed itself.

7th July 1994

Dorothy and I saw the young eagle take its maiden flight early last week. It has been exercising its wings by flapping vigorously and jumping from one edge of the nest to the other for the past several weeks. This time, as we watched through the telescope, it flapped is wings, sailed over the edge of the nest, and became airborne. Flapping rigorously, it landed awkwardly on the limb of a pine tree close by. It was still there and composing itself and looking around when we left.

We took several guests out the next evening and found the nest to be empty, but while we watched, the young eagle came soaring over woods and made a more practiced landing in the big pine near the nest. It sat there, like a blowzy teenager, the wind blowing its feathers as it tried to fold its wings just so, exhibiting none of the trim elegance displayed by its parents.

The parents will continue to feed it at the nest for a month or so, and it will hang out around that area for the rest of the summer as it gradually learns how to hunt for itself. It will spend the next four years wandering up and down the east coast, if all goes well, and will probably return to this area as an adult to breed. Action was taken in time, and our national symbol is coming back from the brink of extinction.

21st July 1994

I got phone calls within hours of each other last week from Billy Pruden and Fred Inglis, who had been cruising some timber that Billy wanted to log and discovered a turkey vulture nest in the base of a hollow tulip poplar. I have been trying to locate and photograph nesting vultures for years, so was quite elated at the news. I met Fred early the next morning and he led me to the nest site. It's on Billy's property, back in an isolated area at the edge of a swamp full of really big tupelo gums.

When we arrived at the nest site, two immature turkey vultures were outside the hollow tree exercising their wings. Upon sighting us they both hopped awkwardly back to the nest tree and up and into the big hole near its base. We peered in and were greeted with a volley of fierce loud hisses. The young vultures, fully feathered but unable to fly, crouched on their bellies and peered up at us. They continued to threaten me with fierce hisses as I took photographs, but they made no attempt to project vomit at me, a common defense of young vultures. I could detect no foul odor around the nest.

Like all young animals and birds, these young vultures projected a soft-eyed, gentle image that made one want to pick them up and cuddle them—an action which would lead to very messy, smelly consequences! It is interesting that the young of all species have the soft, big-eyed, gentle look that make one want to cuddle and protect them, probably a defense mechanism on their part: they are so much trouble to raise that otherwise their parents would abandon them at birth!

The nest itself is inside the hollow base of a very large tulip poplar. The outside of the hollow starts about four feet from the ground and the hollow itself extends up for about eight feet; the inside diameter is about six feet; and the base of the hollow is about two feet below ground level. The adult vultures make no attempt at a nest. They simply lay a pair of eggs, a warm white overlaid with bright brown splotches, directly on the soil and decayed wood at the base of the hollow. Both sexes share in incubation, which lasts for thirty to forty days. Such natural nest sites are quite rare; this one looks as if it has been in use for years, and I hope that if this area has to be logged, the area around the nest tree will not be disturbed.

15th September 1994

As I played down Number 13 fairway last week I put up a sharp-shinned hawk from one of the small hills along the right side. It was feeding on a bird of some kind, so I investigated and found the remains (head, feet, and long tail) of a yellow-billed cuckoo. This very elegant bird is a breeder here but is more often heard than seen.

13th October 1994

I got phone call Monday afternoon from Royster-Clark. They had found an owl in an open pit near one of their storage sheds. The pit had water in it, and the owl was waterlogged and couldn't fly. It didn't seem to be injured or starved, but I put a chicken wing in with it anyway. It sat back, erected its feathers to make it seem as large as a bushel basket, popped its beak, and glared at me with yellow eyes the size of golf balls. I picked it up, dried it off overnight, and released it back at Royster-Clark Tuesday morning.

It was a horned owl, our fiercest and most beautiful owl. As well as being beautiful this is a most useful owl. Big and strong enough to regularly prey on the largest rats, it may catch as many as six each night when it has young. This one is a regular hanger-on at Royster-Clark and has been observed catching rats around the storage building. There are also a lot of feral pigeons around the area, and the owl probably takes some of these as well.

8th December 1994

This time of year with all the gulls in the fields there are invariably a few that will fly in front of cars and become injured. I have had two referred to me already this month. I do not know of anyone in the area who rehabilitates gulls, so the best thing to do if you rescue one is to take it to the waterfront and release it into the water. gulls are tough, hardy birds and their chances of survival are pretty good.

5th January 1995

Driving across the Albemarle Sound Bridge Sunday afternoon, we spotted a peregrine falcon perched on the bridge railing beside our lane. It was a brightly colored male, and he let us slow down and pass him at about seven feet. It is always a thrill to see one of these magnificent birds of prey. Later that afternoon we saw another winging along the lakeshore at Pettigrew State Park. This fastest of all raptors takes ducks and shorebirds, but I suspect that this one will dine heavily on robins; there are literally thousands spending the winter in and around the park.

These same robins passed through the Edenton area almost a month ago, stripping all the berries from the dogwood trees as they passed through. They will spend the rest of the winter in the red-bay thickets along the south side of Lake Phelps, feeding on the berries. mockingbirds probably wish all robins in Hades! Long before the migrating robins arrive, the mockingbirds have each staked out individual winter territories—which invariably include several fruiting dogwoods—and vigorously defend these trees from bluebirds, catbirds, and waxwings. They totally lose out when the robins arrive and descend on their trees. While they are chasing one robin away, hundreds more are busy gobbling fruit; they will strip a tree in the course of a morning's forage.

A big bald eagle is visiting the Commons area along Country Club Drive. I have seen it there two times during the past week.

26th January 1995

It's getting close to the time for eagles to nest again and I have been keeping an eye on their last year's nest. They have added more sticks to it, and I've seen them perched close to the nest but not actually on the nest this year. Logging crews are thinning in the pine woods close by, which is probably disturbing them a bit, but if the logging operations stay away from the immediate area of the nest tree itself and finish up in the next few weeks, I don't think that the eagles will abandon the nest. I think that there is an additional pair of adult eagles in the area this year, and I'm keeping an eye out for a new nesting pair.

There seem to be an unusual number of vultures around this

winter, both the more common turkey vulture and the slightly smaller black vulture. Every evening for the last week they have been establishing roosts in the woods near our house. It's quite a sight to see fifty to sixty big heavy birds with six-foot wingspans come crashing through the branches and settle in for the night.

16th February 1995

I was amused Sunday afternoon out on Drummond Point as I watched a mockingbird successfully defend its fruiting red cedar tree from half a dozen cedar waxwings. The mockingbird would absolutely not let the circling waxwings land in its cedar tree or in any tree close to it. At the same time, it paid no attention to the white-throated sparrows and juncos who sat in the cedar. mockingbirds will drive bluebirds, thrushes, thrashers, and other mockingbirds, and will attempt to drive robins, away from their fruiting trees. I guess they have learned from bitter experience who the fruit thieves are.

23rd March 1995

The sharp-shinned hawks are still with us. I see them lurking around our feeders almost every day. Last week as I was working on a raised bed in Toby's garden on Country Club Drive, I heard a bird's cry of distress and I looked up to see a sharpshin pinning a male cardinal to the ground about fifteen feet away. I waved my arm at it, but it reached forward with its beak, clipped through the cardinal's neck vertebrae, and took off, carrying the cardinal with it. You have to be philosophical about such things and hope that only smart, healthy, male cardinals grow up to become fathers of the next generation.

25th May 1995

The pair of eagles who fledged one young eagle from their nest along Indian Trail Road last year have abandoned that nest this year and built a new one near Fred and Jeannie Inglis's home at Somerset Farm. Fred keeps me informed of their activities, and I can set up a telescope in their front yard and get a pretty good look at the eagles' activity around the nest. They are raising one eaglet again this year. Through the telescope we can see it standing on the rim of the nest, flapping and exercising its long skinny wings.

The turkey vulture has probably hatched her two eggs by now. The last time I checked out her nest I had an eye-to-eye confrontation with her at about four feet. I backed away, still smelling like a rose, and haven't bothered her since. I'll try to go back soon and check the progress of the young vultures.

17th July 1995

It's been a little too hot to do much parking by my little woodland pool to photograph the activity going on there as the water level shrinks in the rest of the stream, but I have spent a little time there in the early mornings. As things quieten down after my arrival, a couple of shy little green-backed herons come in quietly and begin to fish for minnows around the edges of the pool, keeping a wary eye out for cottonmouth moccasins and snapping turtles.

5th October 1995

Sharp-shinned and Cooper's hawks, our earliest migrants, are here in fair numbers right now. These little hawks are bird-killing machines, ruthlessly weeding out the sick and unwary members of our songbird population. Saturday, out on the golf course, I saw a sharpshin catch a mockingbird almost as large as itself. The mockingbird was so busy chasing another mockingbird from its territory that it forgot to stick close to cover—just the kind of situation the sharpshin was evolved to exploit. These hawks are skulkers and you don't see them too often. But neat little piles of feathers in the yards around feeders and on the golf course show that they are around—and busy!

One of our resident hawks, a redtail, has a favorite perch on the wires along Route 32 just before the Pelikan plant. He can be seen there every day, scanning the fields and ditches for mice and rats. This beautiful and beneficial hawk doesn't bother birds, but will take squirrels; occasionally one will take up residence in town and become a pigeon specialist.

There have been quite a few eagle sightings this fall. Fred Inglis saw three immatures several weeks ago. I saw two immature ones in the same area a week later, and Jay Underhill reported an adult flying past his place last week.

9th November 1995

I am always amazed at the number of species of birds that live or forage in our small towns and in the suburbs of our large cities. Here in the South if there is enough cover in trees and shrubs, every yard will have its resident pair of mockingbirds, robins, and perhaps catbirds. Blue jays and house finches are much more common in town than in our woods. Even during fall migration a lot of birds forage through the yards, gardens, and street trees.

Last week Dorothy had to deliver a package to Morris Circle. I drove her over and sat in the car waiting for her. Lots of little birds in the live oak overhead attracted my attention, so I rolled down the car window and spished softly to get their attention. They were a mixed flock of wood warblers. I saw one black-throated blue and one pine warbler; the rest, as far as I could see, were yellow-rumped warblers, quite fearless. They hovered within arm's reach, trying to figure out what the fuss was all about. yellow-rumped warblers are such suckers for spishing that I can call all within earshot to me in a few minutes.

I continue to get sighting reports on the eagles over the Yeopim River and out at Drummond Point. Last week Sid Shearin reported a pair of mature bald eagles perched in a big cypress along Newland Road at about the same spot that Frances and Fred Inglis and I saw them on last year's Christmas Bird Count. I will look around over in that area to see if we have a new nest site nearby.

ADVENTURES WITH BIRDS

30th November 1995

I am keeping a log of eagle sightings in the area for eagle projects that the State is conducting with timber companies in the area. Weekly sightings of eagles are being reported from the Drummond Point area and along the Yeopim River. There are mixed reports of a pair of adult eagles and at least three immatures. Jay Underhill reported an immature with a partial white head just off his dock last week. It plucked a fish from the water and perched in a tree by the Woods' dock to eat. The partial white head would make it about three years old and about ready to breed. It will be looking for a mate and territory in the area during the next two years.

On November 23rd I observed a pair of mature bald eagles just south of the Newland Road in Washington County. They were flying very low and slow over about a mile-long territory along the edge of the Tyson Farms. They lit in a tree fairly close to the road and I got several photos. The female was huge, at least a third larger than her consort. This is the third time this year the pair has been reported in this area, so a nest close by is a distinct possibility.

14th December 1995

Now is a pleasant time to take a break from Christmas shopping and take a drive over to Lake Mattamuskeet. There are lots of swans and ducks to see from the causeway and the drive to the headquarters. You may even see an eagle or two—and all from a nice warm car!

25th January 1996

Adult eagles are active around last year's nest, and if they are not disturbed they will probably nest there again this year.

Saw some interesting behavior I've never seen before by a large flock of cedar waxwings last Sunday afternoon near the Lodge at Lake Mattamuskeet. They would all be feeding on red cedar berries when suddenly they all flew straight down to shallow water in the canal, lit on the surface with rapidly fluttering wings for a second or two, then back up into the tree, only to repeat the maneuver in a few seconds. It looked as if they were getting a drink and taking a bath at the same time.

8th February 1996

Sunday afternoon, along Indian Trail Road I saw a group of turkey vultures resting in a tree near the road. I turned around at an intersection, drove slowly, and was able to park off the road about forty yards from the vultures and observe them for several hours. There were only four there at first, but they kept dropping in by twos and threes until by the time I left there were forty-three of them, all turkey vultures except for a group of seven black vultures who came in a group. Vulture eyesight is phenomenal. I could see vultures as small specks on the horizon, all heading for the meeting in the tree by the car.

At this time of year they are re-cementing pair bonds, and there was quite a bit of aerial activity. A pair would fly in circles at about fifteen hundred feet, when the upper one would half close its wings and execute a power dive at the one below it, pulling out at the last minute; the sound of the air rushing through its stiffened wings sounded like ripping cloth. For such large birds they show an astonishing amount of grace and power. After a few of these passes they would drop into the tree, sidle along the branch, and proceed to groom each other's head and neck feathers.

Graceful in flight, they are very clumsy while perching and maneuvering in the trees. Black vultures did not engage in any aerial acrobatics but pairs also began mutual grooming after landing. Black vultures are marginally less awkward in the trees than the turkey vultures.

18th April 1996

While visiting their grandparents in Edenton, Ollie and Hazel Inglis found a headless marsh bird near the gate in the side yard.

Frances called me and we determined that it was a clapper rail, probably caught by an owl or cat who will often just eat the heads of their prey.

9th May 1996

As I was standing chatting in the parking lot at the Edenton post office, I noticed a lot of large birds wheeling in circles high up, five to six thousand feet. Through the binoculars I could see that they were what hawk watchers call a "kettle"—a group of hawks of various species on migration who have found a thermal and wheel within it, rising to impressive heights before the thermal dissipates and they boil off in a long down-sloping glide north to find another thermal and repeat the process. Hawks hate to expend energy by flapping while on migration and are constantly on the lookout for thermals to get a free lift. It's unusual to see them here though; they prefer to use well established routes along mountain ridges where uplifts are more common. This kettle had red-tailed, red-shouldered, broad-winged, and several accipiters, sharp-shinned or Cooper's hawks.

23rd May 1996

On Saturday morning I parked the car off the road where Lakeshore Drive crosses the upper end of Queen Anne's Creek and was watching for activity in the side with flooded dead trees. A pileated woodpecker flew towards me from farther back in the swamp and landed about four feet above the water on the trunk of a flooded tree. It spiraled down the trunk towards the water, to get a drink I thought. Suddenly it hopped back up about a foot and, cocking its head from side to side in an agitated fashion, it began to watch something in the water very closely. Through the binoculars I could see the source of its interest: a cottonmouth about twenty inches long was coiled on a root at water level. A snake this size wouldn't have any interest in a bird the size of a pileated, but the big woodpecker kept hopping around until it put the snake to flight. As the snake swam from tree trunk to tree trunk, the pileated followed, not getting too close but definitely interested. After about ten minutes the snake went into a hole at the base of a dead tree and the pileated lost interest and flew off through the swamp towards Hayes.

Audubon
Christmas Bird Counts

DECEMBER, THE MONTH OF CHRISTMAS,
and, for birders, the month of the annual bird count. Each holiday season more than 43,000 people from Alaska to Brazil spend one winter day counting and recording birds as part of the National Audubon Christmas Bird Count.

These are held nationwide during a two-week period centered on Christmas Day. The rules are very specific: a fifteen-mile-diameter circle is drawn on a map around a local landmark such as a church or post office; parties of birders are assigned parts of the circle, and walk and drive through their assigned area listing all the species of birds and the number of individuals of each species seen during a twenty-four-hour period ; at the end of the day everyone meets at a member's house or an area restaurant to warm up, socialize, and compile a master list which is forwarded to the National Audubon Society.

It's a lot of fun, and when the counts are in adjacent communities, a spirited rivalry usually develops as to who sees the most species. The lists are usually published in a local paper so everyone can see who's the best in any given year. The fee is $5 per birder, and Audubon uses this fee to print the results in a special issue of *American Birds*. The names of all participants are listed in the book.

The Christmas Counts have a serious purpose in addition to the fun one. Being essentially at the top of the food chain, through their diet birds accumulate in their tissues the pesticides and chemicals that are loose in the air, soil, and water, and thus are one of the most sensitive biological indicators of the quality of our environment. The Audubon society keeps an up-to-date computerized list of all the Christmas Counts, and when a species shows a downward population trend it sounds an alert. This might indicate a serious environmental pollution problem, and wildlife biologists begin to investigate to find the reason for the decline.

There are Christmas Counts in Pamlico, Goose Creek State Park, Nags Head, Pea Island, and at Lake Mattamuskeet. The local count is the Pettigrew Christmas Bird Count, held each year around 28th December in a fifteen-mile radius of Pettigrew State Park. Participants meet at the Park office at 6:30 AM, come rain or shine, and are invited to my home that evening for corn chowder, socializing, and compilation.

1985

Today Matt, and I took part in our first North Carolina Christmas Bird Count. It took place in a fifteen-mile diameter circle centered on the headquarters at the Mattamuskeet National Wildlife Refuge.

We left home at about 4:30 AM so we would arrive at the headquarters and get a chance to listen for owls. We joined Mike and Jan Dunn and Grace Smith, and were assigned a quadrant that included the causeway across the lake and a section around the northeastern edge. Mike had a tape recording of owl calls, and we stopped at a dense patch of woods and played the calls. After about three minutes of playing the screech-owl recording we had two screech-owls up close—one on each side of the road and each vigorously challenging the supposed intruder. (Incidentally, "screech" owl seems a misnomer, for the calls are low and melodious.) The barred owl recording elicited a response from a local barred owl and also stimulated a great horned owl into vocal activity. Our three owls properly recorded, we went out onto the causeway and began recording waterfowl species and numbers.

Recording species was easy, but counting the thousands of ducks, geese, and swans was a chore that took up most of the morning. Also seen from the causeway were four bald eagles, two immatures and two adults. We set up powerful spotting scopes, and several carloads of tourists and casual birders were able to get their first close-up look at the mature bald eagle.

We worked our way around the lake, splashing through reed beds and spishing up marsh wrens, sedge wrens, and sparrow species to add to our growing list. Halfway around our quadrant we came across a birder who was stopped beside the road looking intently through binoculars into a field of very large pigs. We stopped, as all birders do when they see another birder looking at something, and saw a real rarity, perhaps a first for North

Carolina. It was identified first as a western kingbird, a bird of the midwest and western region, but when word spread and the deadly serious "big-bore" birders showed up, a lively discussion developed. Everyone agreed that it was not a western kingbird. One group said it was a Cassin's kingbird, whose range is in the southwest and Mexico. A second group said it was a tropical kingbird, whose range is in western Mexico. The third group said Couch's kingbird, which ranges in eastern Mexico.

When the count was over we tabulated our counts but did not stay for the dinner. When we left the discussion was still hot and heavy about the kingbird, with half a dozen different bird guides open on the table and several phones busy talking with out-of-state experts on Mexican birds. The controversy was finally settled in favor of the tropical kingbird. I don't know if any blood was shed during the decision-making, but serious birders are very serious about their avocation!

Our group counted 84 species of birds, with the total number of individuals in the thousands. The total count of all the groups combined will probably be around 130 species and total individuals around 130,000.

1986

On Sunday December 21st nine birders and myself met at dawn at the Pettigrew State Park headquarters and inaugurated the first Pettigrew State Park Christmas Bird Count. Ten birders are not very many to cover 176 square miles, and I would like to get more local people involved. I must admit to a curiosity about why in a town the size of Edenton there are not more (*any?*) active birders.

We split into three groups for the morning and fanned out around the lake and across the countryside. We all met back at the Park Headquarters where we sat in the sun out of the wind, compared notes, and ate lunch. We split up again and covered as much territory as we could before dark, then all met at my house at 6 PM for socializing, eating hot corn chowder, comparing notes, and compiling the bird list.

For ten observers we had a very good count, sighting 85 different species and 21,521 individual birds. To put this in perspective, in 1985 the count in the Atlantic area of the Panama Canal scored the highest, with 324 species; the highest in the US was Freeport, Texas with 207 species. At the low end, a friend of mine in Deering, Alaska conducted his Christmas count in minus thirty degree weather and found only two species: common raven and snow bunting!

1987

On sunny days most counts have plenty of observers, but as the weather worsens the number of observers drops, and in a driving rain or snow storm only the most nitty-gritty, dedicated birders stick it out. It's lucky we had enough of them to go round this year, because it rained half a day on the Pettigrew Count, three-quarters of a day on the Mattamuskeet Count, and all day on the Goose Creek Count. In general, birds are less active in bad weather and it takes more searching to find them. The observers, their binoculars, glasses, and notebooks all get wet, and the back roads and logging roads (the most productive) become muddy and impassible.

The presence of good, dedicated birders is what makes a count a success, and we need more of them. We had nine for the Pettigrew Count and tallied 85 species of birds, including an immature bald eagle and a real rarity, a peregrine falcon. The Mattamuskeet Count probably had in excess of twenty participants and got a total of 109 species. Matt and I counted 85 species in our sector, including three immature bald eagles. I think I got several good photographs of one of them. The Goose Creek Count had about eighteen observers and the species tally will be around 92–95 species.

In the migratory songbird group the most numerous species in our count areas was the American robin, followed by the white-throated sparrow, the junco, and the song sparrow. With our local nesting species, the titmice were the most numerous, followed by Carolina chickadees and bluebirds. The most numerous warbler, hands down, was the yellow-rumped warbler, which was everywhere.

1988

Matt and I took part in three local counts this year. The first was at Goose Creek State Park on December 18th. We had better weather this year and a better count, with a total of 101 species seen. The high point for me was the sighting of a red-cockaded woodpecker in a pine forest. The second count was the Mattamuskeet Count on December 28th. Mattamuskeet is always an interesting place to visit, with thousands upon thousands of ducks, geese, and swans who let you get quite close. My group of four people saw a total of 102 species. We were unable to stay for the final count, but I would guess that the total would be around 115–120 species.

Our own count took place at Pettigrew State Park on December 30th. I am compiler for this count and I know everyone who took part. Of the sixteen of us, four were from Columbia, two from Creswell, and two from Edenton (Matt and me!). I know that there are a lot of interested people out there because they read my column and I get a lot of feedback. I would simply like to get more local people actively involved. Everyone had a good time in the field, and we returned to my house in the evening for hot corn chowder and socializing. We observed a total of 104 species, the most we have ever seen in the Pettigrew Count area. Regretfully, we could not count in the total the seven black bears that came within fifty yards of one party!

One of the rarer birds seen on the count was a goshawk, the largest North American accipiter, usually a denizen of the northern forests but sometimes seen in our mountains in the winter.

RED-COCKADED WOODPECKER
Picoides borealis

I have seen this one three times during the last month, in the pine and bay forests along the south shore of Lake Phelps. There are a lot of robins and mourning doves in the area, and I think that the hawk has been catching and eating them. It is quite wary and I have not been able to photograph it so far.

1989

This was the 90th Annual Audubon Christmas Bird Count, held this year during the period from December 16th through January 3rd. I took part in four counts this year: the Goose Creek Park Count, with 105 species including a small band of red-cockaded woodpeckers, a rare and endangered species; the Mattamuskeet Count; the Pettigrew State Park Count, with 104 species; and the Rocky Mount Count.

During the count period this year, Lake Mattamuskeet was frozen solid, and I saw only a small percentage of the waterfowl that we normally have there. Lake Phelps was also frozen over, but it had an area at the eastern end which remained open. A lot of geese and swans that would have normally been on Lake Mattamuskeet came to Lake Phelps instead. Last year we had a total of about 38,000 individuals; this year we had over 255,000.

1990

This year we counted 104 species on our Pettigrew State Park Count. Texas and California counts always come up with 200 plus species, and Panama is usually the champion with over 300 species. At the other end of the scale was Point Barrow, Alaska, with a count of nine birds—all ravens!

1991

Our Audubon Christmas Bird Counts are over for another year. We had nine people for our local count, and did very well, tallying a total of 96 species, including an immature bald eagle.

I participated in the Beaufort County Count as well this year, and had rather a pleasant day although the count was down from last year. Talking with other people on the count, I found that their impression too is that there are fewer birds coming to their feeders so far this fall. The count tallied 84 species this year against 89 last year, and the total numbers of birds were down as well. In particular the count for cardinals was way down, and this correlates with the total absence of cardinals at my feeder so far this fall. Normally I would have had half a dozen pairs.

What concerns me most is that the birds that are absent from my feeders and other feeders in the Coastal Plain this year are birds like cardinals, titmice, chickadees, and woodpeckers—birds that breed here and do not migrate. Birds are an excellent indicator of the quality of our environment, and if their numbers fall drastically then we had better find out why—and quickly!

1992

Our 1992 Pettigrew Christmas Bird Count went off quite well, despite a steady all-day rain. We tallied 105 species and over 36,000 individual birds. We had, in addition to myself from Edenton, birders from Creswell, Columbia, Greenville, Roanoke Rapids, and Raleigh.

We got two endangered species this year, a peregrine falcon and a bald eagle, and in addition another species which, while it has probably the widest worldwide distribution, is becoming rare in North Carolina: the common barn-owl.

1993

Our annual count at Pettigrew State Park was held on December 29th and coincided with a big freezing rain and ice storm. Some of our regular participants could not make it through the storm, so we were short-handed this year. A lot of our farm roads were impassable, and we did not have enough birders to cover all of our territory. In the afternoon fog settled in, limiting visibility on land and making it impossible to see anything on Lake Phelps. Quite the worst conditions for a bird census that I've experienced in about fifteen years.

Dogged persistence paid off, however, and we ended up with

a tally of 91 species of birds seen. With good weather we could have expected to see about 103 species, our tally last year. We didn't come up with any great rarities on the count, but did see over 50 common loons on Lake Phelps before the fog closed in. In a farmer's field in Cherry we counted 75 American pipits, and I looked at every one hoping for a horned lark or a longspur, who often occur in mixed flocks with pipits, but no luck this year. We saw two evening grosbeaks, birds who usually stay farther north and are not seen on our counts.

1994

We had a beautiful day for this year's Pettigrew Count and, despite a shortage of participants, tallied a respectable count of 99 species. The best birds this year were all raptor species: two mature bald eagles, one peregrine falcon, and one merlin.

The last few years of counts have shown an alarming drop in the populations of our deciduous woodland birds—the warblers, thrushes, and vireos—and several programs have been started, both here and on the birds' wintering grounds, to try to find the reason for the precipitous decline.

1995

An interesting and successful Audubon Christmas Bird Count on December 28th, tallying a total of 102 bird species. It was a beautiful day, cold but clear, and everyone had a good time. Notable species seen were two bald eagles, a white-fronted goose, a Ross' goose, a Le Conte's sparrow, and 33 short-eared owls.

A big flock of these owls has been reported as being on the Tyson corporate farm for the last four years, but this year was the first sighting for our Christmas count. One of the eagles was an immature one, and it was seen at four different times and places around Phelps Lake, once feeding on a sizable fish. We also found three dead swans, evidence suggesting that they had been killed by an eagle.

Post Script

I HAVE BECOME QUITE DISMAYED by the tunnel vision of our species. We are not alone on this planet. The earth is a vast balanced system that is slowly evolving. Along with all the other animals and plants, we are a part of that system; everything is tied to everything else in ways that we do not fully understand. Yet for short-term gains we tinker with a system that works, one we are dependent upon for our very existence. This is a recipe for disaster, and it is the reason for the activities of many people worldwide—including me—who are attempting to sound a "wake-up call."

I am always sad that we do not get any young birders on our bird counts. The human race desperately needs the next generation to be interested, knowledgeable, and concerned about the deteriorating quality of our environment. If it is not, and we continue to pollute and poison our water and air as we and our predecessors have done, we may find that, having driven many other species to extinction, we are not sacred or immune as a species ourselves. We won't destroy the earth. Mother Earth will simply take a few million years to rid herself of poisons and will start over again, crossing out intelligence as a viable option.

FROM HAWKS TO HUMMINGBIRDS

Birds of the Area

Anhinga
Anhinga anhinga
Avocet, American
Recurvirostra americana
Bittern, American
Botaurus lentiginosus
Bittern, Least
Ixobrychus exilis
Blackbird, Red-winged
Agelaius phoeniceus
Bluebird, Eastern
Sialia sialis
Bobolink
Dolichonyx oryzivorus
Bunting, Indigo
Passerina cyanea
Canvasback
Aythya valisineria
Cardinal, Northern
Cardinalis cardinalis
Catbird, Grey
Dumetella carolinensis
Chat, Yellow-breasted
Icteria virens
Chickadee, Carolina
Parus carolinensis

Chuck-will's-widow
Caprimulgus carolinensis
Coot, American
Fulica americana
Cormorant, Double-crested
Phalacrocorax auritus
Cowbird, Brown-headed
Molothrus ater
Creeper, Brown
Certhia americana
Crow, American
Corvus brachyrhynchos
Crow, Fish
Corvus ossifragus
Cuckoo, Yellow-billed
Coccyzus americanus
Dove, Mourning
Zenaida macroura
Dove, Rock
Columba livia
Duck, Black
Anas rubripes
Duck, Harlequin
Histrionicus histrionicus
Duck, Ring-necked
Aythya collaris

Duck, Ruddy
  Oxyura jamaicensis
Duck, Wood
  Aix sponsa
Eagle, Bald
  Haliaeetus leucocephalus
Eagle, Golden
  Aquila chrysaetos
Egret, Cattle
  Bubulcus ibis
Egret, Common
  Casmerodius albus
Eider, Common
  Somateria mollissima
Eider, King
  Somateria spectablis
Falcon, Peregrine
  Falco peregrinus
Finch, House
  Carpodacus mexicanus
Finch, Purple
  Carpodacus purpureus
Flicker, Northern
  Colaptes auratus
Flycatcher, Acadian
  Empidonax virescens
Flycatcher, Great-crested
  Myiarchus crinitus
Gannet, Northern
  Sula bassanus
Gnatcatcher, Blue-gray
  Polioptila caerulea
Goldfinch
  Carduelis tristis
Goose, Blue
  see Snow Goose

Goose, Canada
  Branta canadensis
Goose, Greater White-fronted
  Anser albifrons
Goose, Ross'
  Chen rossii
Goose, Snow
  Chen caerulescens
Goshawk, Northern
  Accipiter gentilis
Grackle, Common
  Quiscalus quiscula
Grebe, Horned
  Podiceps auritus
Grebe, Pied-billed
  Podilymbus podiceps
Grosbeak, Blue
  Guiraca caerulea
Grosbeak, Evening
  Coccothraustes vespertinus
Grouse, Ruffed
  Bonasa umbellus
Gull, Bonaparte's
  Larus philadelphia
Gull, Great Black-backed
  Larus marinus
Gull, Herring
  Larus argentatus
Gull, Laughing
  Larus atricilla
Gull, Lesser Black-backed
  Larus fuscus
Gull, Little
  Larus minutus
Gull, Ring-billed
  Larus delawarensis

Harrier, Northern
Circus cyaneus
Hawk, Broad-winged
Buteo platypterus
Hawk, Cooper's
Accipiter cooperii
Hawk, Duck
see Peregrine Falcon
Hawk, Marsh
see Northern Harrier
Hawk, Pigeon
see Merlin
Hawk, Red-shouldered
Buteo lineatus
Hawk, Red-tailed
Buteo jamaicensis
Hawk, Sharp-shinned
Accipiter striatus
Hawk, Sparrow
see American Kestrel
Heron, Great Blue
Ardea herodias
Heron, Green-backed
Butorides striatus
Heron, Little Blue
Egretta caerulea
Hummingbird, Black-chinned
Archilocus alexandri
Hummingbird, Ruby-throated
Archilocus colubris
Hummingbird, Rufous
Selasphorus rufus
Goldfinch, American
Carduelis tristis
Ibis, Glossy
Plegadis falcinellus

Jay, Blue
Cyanocitta cristata
Junco, Dark-eyed
Junco hyemalis
Kestrel, American
Falco sparverius
Killdeer
Charadrius vociferus
Kingbird, Cassin's
Tyrannus vociferans
Kingbird, Couch's
Tyrannus couchii
Kingbird, Tropical
Tyrannus melancholicus
Kingbird, Western
Tyrannus verticalis
Kinglet, Gold-crowned
Regulus satrapa
Kinglet, Ruby-crowned
Regulus calendula
Lark, Horned
Eremophila alpestris
Loon, Common
Gavia immer
Mallard
Anas platyrhynchos
Martin, Purple
Progne subis
Meadowlark, Eastern
Sturnella magna
Merganser, Common
Mergus merganser
Merganser, Hooded
Lophodytes cucullatus
Merganser, Red-breasted
Mergus serrator

Merlin
Falco columbarius
Mockingbird, Northern
Mimus polyglottos
Nighthawk, Common
Chordeiles minor
Nuthatch, Brown-headed
Sitta pusilla
Nuthatch, Red-breasted
Sitta canadensis
Nuthatch, White-breasted
Sitta carolinensis
Oriole, Orchard
Icterus spurius
Osprey
Pandion haliaetus
Ovenbird
Seiurus aurocapillus
Owl, Barred
Strix varia
Owl, Common Barn-
Tyto alba
Owl, Eastern Screech-
Otus asio
Owl, Great Horned
Bubo virginianus
Owl, Short-eared
Asio flammeus
Parula, Northern
Parula americana
Pelican, Brown
Pelecanus occidentalis
Pelican, White
Pelecanus erythrorhynchos
Phoebe, Eastern
Sayornis phoebe

Pipit, American
Anthus rubescens
Quail, Northern
Colinus virginianus
Quail, Scaled
Callipepla squamata
Rail, Clapper
Rallus longirostris
Rail, Virginia
Rallus limicola
Redstart, American
Setophaga ruticilla
Robin, American
Turdus migratorius
Sandpiper, Solitary
Tringa solitaria
Shoveler, Northern
Anas clypeata
Snakebird
see Anhinga
Sparrow, American Tree
Spizella arborea
Sparrow, Chipping
Spizella passerina
Sparrow, Fox
Passerella iliaca
Sparrow, Le Conte's
Ammodramus leconteii
Sparrow, Song
Melospiza melodia
Sparrow, Swamp
Melospiza georgiana
Sparrow, White-crowned
Zonotrichia leucophrys
Sparrow, White-throated
Zonotrichia albicollis

Starling, European
Sturnus vulgaris
Swallow, Barn
Hirundo rustica
Swallow, Northern Rough-winged
Stelgidopteryx serripennis
Swallow, Tree
Tachycineta bicolor
Swan, Black
Cygnus atratus
Swan, Tundra
Cygnus columbianus
Swift, Chimney
Chaetura pelagica
Tanager, Scarlet
Piranga olivacea
Tanager, Summer
Piranga rubra
Teal, Green-winged
Anas crecca
Tern, Caspian
Sterna caspia
Tern, Forster's
Sterna forsteri
Thrasher, Brown
Toxostoma rufum
Thrush, Hermit
Catharus guttatus
Thrush, Wood
Hylocichla mustelina
Titmouse, Tufted
Parus bicolor
Towhee, Rufous-sided
Pipilo erythrophthalmus
Turkey, Water
see Anhinga

Turkey, Wild
Meleagris gallopavo
Vireo, Red-eyed
Vireo olivaceus
Vireo, Warbling
Vireo gilvus
Vireo, White-eyed
Vireo griseus
Vulture, Black
Coragyps atratus
Vulture, Turkey
Cathartes aura
Warbler, Bachman's
Vermivora bachmanii
Warbler, Black-and-white
Mniotilta varia
Warbler, Black-throated Blue
Dendroica caerulescens
Warbler, Black-throated Green
Dendroica virens
Warbler, Orange-crowned
Vermivora celata
Warbler, Palm
Dendroica palmarum
Warbler, Pine
Dendroica pinus
Warbler, Prairie
Dendroica discolor
Warbler, Prothonotary
Protonotaria citrea
Warbler, Wilson's
Wilsonia pusilla
Warbler, Yellow
Dendroica petechia
Warbler, Yellow-rumped
Dendroica coronata

Warbler, Yellow-throated
Dendroica dominica

Waterthrush, Louisiana
Seiurus motacilla

Waxwing, Bohemian
Bombycilla garrulus

Waxwing, Cedar
Bombycilla cedrorum

Whip-poor-will
Caprimulgus vociferus

Wigeon, Eurasian
Anas penelope

Wood-Pewee, Eastern
Contopus virens

Woodcock, American
Scolopax minor

Woodpecker, Acorn
Melanerpes formicivorus

Woodpecker, Downy
Picoides pubescens

Woodpecker, Hairy
Picoides villosus

Woodpecker, Pileated
Dryocopus pileatus

Woodpecker, Red-bellied
Melanerpes carolinus

Woodpecker, Red-cockaded
Picoides borealis

Wren, Carolina
Thryothorus ludovicianus

Wren, House
Troglodytes aedon

Wren, Marsh
Cistothorus palustris

Wren, Sedge
Cistothorus platensis

Wren, Winter
Troglodytes troglodytes

Yellowthroat, Common
Geothlypis trichas

Useful Addresses

Ahoskie Animal Hospital
Route 4, Box 52, Ahoskie, NC 27910
telephone: 919/332-6179

Alligator River National Wildlife Refuge
along US 64/264 west of Manteo
telephone: 919/473-1131

Cape Hatteras Bird Club
PO Box 895, Buxton, NC 27920

Carolina Bird Club Inc.
PO Box 29555, Raleigh, NC 27626-0555

Carolina Raptor Center
PO Box 16443, Charlotte, NC 28297
telephone: 704/875-6521

Chowan Herald
421 South Broad Street, Edenton, NC 27932
telephone: 919/482-4418

Goose Creek State Park
2190 Camp Leach Road, Washington, NC 27889
telephone: 919/923-2191

Greenville Bird Club
PO Box 7202, Greenville, NC 27835

Keel's Critter Clinic
(small animals, cattle, exotics, wildlife, rarities, etc)
503 North Main Street, Robersonville, NC 27871
telephone: 919/795-4445

Mattamuskeet National Wildlife Refuge
Route 1, Box N-2, Swan Quarter, NC 27885
telephone: 919/926-4021

Merchants Millpond State Park
Route 1, Box 141A, Gatesville, NC 27938
telephone: 919/357-1191

Nag's Head Woods Preserve
701 West Ocean Acres Drive, Kill Devil Hills, NC 27948
telephone: 919/441-2525

NC Department of Natural Resources
Division of Parks and Recreation
PO Box 27687, Raleigh, NC 27611-7687
telephone: 919/733-PARK

North Carolina Nature Conservancy
4011 University Drive, Suite 201, Durham, NC 27707
telephone: 919/403-8558

North Carolina Museum of Natural Science
PO Box 29555, Raleigh, NC 27626
telephone: 919/733-7450

Partnership for the Sounds
PO Box 55, Columbia, NC 27925
telephone: 919/796-1000

USEFUL ADDRESSES

Pea Island National Wildlife Refuge
3.5 miles south of Oregon Inlet, next Hwy 12
telephone: 919/473-1131

Pettigrew State Park
2252 Lake Shore Road, Creswell, NC 27928
telephone: 919/797-4475

Pocosin Lakes National Wildlife Refuge
3255 Shore Drive, Creswell, NC 27928
telephone: 919/797-4431

Rare Bird Alert
(information about rare bird sightings across the state)
telephone: 704/332-2473

Roanoke Beacon
PO Box 726, 210 West Water Street, Plymouth, NC 27962
telephone: 919/793-2123

US Fish and Wildlife Service
PO Box 1969, Manteo, NC 27954
telephone: 919/473-1131